Lord is Boaz Lost?

Or Am I

Just In The Wrong Field?

Olivia Stith

Edited by *Kimberly T. Matthews*

LORD IS BOAZ LOST? OR AM I JUST IN THE WRONG FIELD?

All scripture quotations, unless otherwise indicated, are taken from the HOLY BIBLE, NEW INTERNATIONAL VERSION®. NIV®. Copyright © 1973, 1978, 1984 by International Bible Society. Used by permission of Zondervan. All rights reserved.

LORD IS BOAZ LOST? OR AM I JUST IN THE WRONG FIELD?

TriManna Publishing House
New York, NYEmail:
trimannapublishing@gmail.com

Olivia Stith

LORD IS BOAZ LOST? OR AM I JUST IN THE WRONG FIELD? Copyright © 2009 by Olivia Stith. All rights reserved. Printed in the United States of America. No part of this book may be used or reproduced in any manner whatsoever without written permission except in brief quotations embodied in critical articles and reviews. For more information please contact TriManna Publishing House, New York, NY via email at: trimannapublishing@gmail.com

TriManna Publishing House books may be purchased for educational, business, or sales promotional use. For more information please contact TriManna Publishing House, New York, NY via email at: trimannapublishing@gmail.com

Designed by Brittani Williams

ISBN: 978-0-9790603-5-9

Table of Contents

A Word from Elder Olivia Stith

Prologue: Tell the Truth Ruth

Journey of Faith I – Moab Fields: No Man Land

Chapter 1 – Leave Them Heathen Ways Alone

Chapter 2 – When Church Men Make You Sick

Chapter 3 – All Sisters Can't Roll with You

Chapter 4 – Old Wives Tell No Tales: Connecting to Your Naomi

Journey of Faith II – Bethlehem Fields: Working For Boaz

Chapter 5 – You Gotta Work It Sister

Olivia Stith

Chapter 6 – Get the Right Field of Things

Chapter 7 – Who is that Girl!!!

Chapter 8 – Young at Heart and Old in Spirit

Chapter 9 – Girl, Folks Been Talking

Journey of Faith III – Bethlehem: Something Fields Right

Chapter 10 – He Has You Covered Before Becoming Your Covering

Chapter 11 – It's Time to Roll With His Peeps

Chapter 12 – Favor is Just Not Fair!

Chapter 13 – A Little Dip and Sip Will Do

Chapter 14 – He's a Behind The Scenes Man

Chapter 15 – Girlfriend I See a Change

Chapter 16 – Geesh, Now You Tell Me

Chapter 17 – My Lips are Sealed

Journey of Faith IV – Bethlehem: Field – In For One Another

Chapter 18 – Let Wisdom Dress You

Chapter 19 – Feet Don't Fail Me Now

Chapter 20 – Laying Down with Nothing, Getting Up With Everything!

Chapter 21 – Is Patience Part of Your Virtue?

Chapter 22 – No Man Can Stand In His Shoes

Chapter 23 – A Promise Fulfilled

Olivia Stith

Chapter 24 – In The Field Til the Change Comes

10 Thoughts to Ponder

Acknowledgments

I must give the glory and praise to the heavenly Father above, my Lord and Savior Jesus Christ, and the blessed Holy Spirit. My mind could not begin to fathom a word to write without your divine guidance. Thank you for loving me when I was in a Moab and empowering me when I came into my Bethlehem. I praise you God!

My children, Chandler, Taylor and Courtney, you are the extensions of my life. Thank you for your patience, love and (even headaches) which cause me to sit and write for hours. You keep me motivated and on my knees! (Smile)

My parents, Robert and Carolyn Davis who just have been there for me, book after book. It's a blessing to have parents pushing you when you want to just stop and give up. I owe you so much, and I pray that God rewards you both!

My natural sisters, Vickie Deloatch and Erika Davis, and the spiritual ones , Pastor

Olivia Stith

Genifer Pickett, Sandra Boykin and so many more…I can't list you all but you know who you are. I couldn't ask for better sisters who fight for me tooth and nail in the natural and spiritual. Your prayers, encouragements, laughs and jokes keep those dry moments alive!

My second parents, Pal, Lougenia, Bubby and Juanita. Thanks for keeping me in check even when I want to resist

To my spiritual daughter, Melissa Johnson, I am so proud to call you my daughter and be able to see how God is producing great fruit in your life. God truly used you to be a handmaiden in the birthing of this book.

To Kimberly T. Matthews, my editor, who allowed the Spirit to perfect the words of the message. Thank you for laboring with me and trusting in the God we serve.

To my awesome graphic designer, Brittani Williams, thanks for being

patient with me day after day and giving this book your artistic touch.

To all the family - the Stiths' and Davis', and friends, readers and ministries who just have reached out and touched my heart through your support, especially my brothers, Gregory Turner and Brian Henderson who give me the best promotional air time in the world. Thanks for believing in what God has called me to do.

Finally to my Boaz…until we meet in the natural, I pray God continues to strengthen and empower you in the spirit. Soon…soon I believe - real soon we shall meet.

Olivia Stith

Dedication

This book is dedicated to all sisters and brothers whose spiritual journey is that of Ruth and Boaz. May God's hands continually lead you one to the other.

A Prayer for Guidance

Dear Father, in the name of your Son, Jesus, we come to you on the behalf of the sister who is reading this book today. Father, we ask you to please let your Holy Spirit guide her as she seeks your truths in being found by the one you have ordained for her in marriage. We come against any principality or demonic assignments that will attempt to keep the two from meeting. Dear Lord, we are trusting and believing that you will put them on the right path and order their steps so that all things will come together for your glory. We thank you Lord for allowing us to be in your presence and will ask that you continue to keep us under your wings. We trust and believe dear Lord that in your due season you will bring the two together for eternity.

We count it all done in Jesus name.

Amen

Olivia Stith

A Word from Elder Olivia Stith

I praise God for you all. After writing my first relationship book *"If God Is My Lover…Why Is My Bed So Cold?"* which dealt with preparing for your mate, there was a need to further discuss the transitional process of being found by him. Thus, God has blessed me to write, *"Lord is Boaz Lost…Or Am I Just in the Wrong Field?"* I am blessed to be a vessel and share His vision with you.

Understand that *finding* love is not part of God's plan for us, but possessing the love within us and sharing it with someone He sends is. For it is not God's will to hold any good thing or man (smile) from you – He wants us to be in holy unions with men who will cherish and honor us as daughters of the King.

Before you delve into the pages of this book, I strongly advise you to get your Bible and read the Book of Ruth. God has so much He wants to show you within these pages; you will have knowledge of Ruth and Boaz's story, which will enable you to better grasp the concepts in this book.

So, I ask you to pick up your bibles and read. Pray, as you read each chapter, that God shows you what you need to grasp from His Word. God is faithful to those who seek Him with expectancy. Seek Him with a pure heart and He will give you the man of your dreams.

May God continue to bless you all and keep you under His wings.

Kingdom Blessings,

Livi Stith

Olivia Stith

Prologue: Tell the Truth Ruth

Dry, dead, and lifeless are a few words that most would use to describe a desert. For me, those words also describe past relationships I've experienced in the world and even inside the church walls. These relationships left me seeking, desiring and thirsting for more out of life. Lord knows I had been pacing the floors wondering where my Boaz was and even looking at the faces of strange men as they walked by, and whispering or thinking, "Lord is that him? Or is that him? Maybe that's him over there!" I had some serious issues with being single, and scrambled to find relief for my spiritually drought soul. In my heart, I knew there had to be a key - a key that I didn't have – to being in position for my soul mate.

Well the Spirit who loves giving me "Livi catch this" talks opened my eyes one day. I was led to read the book of Ruth from beginning to end. I was told not only to read it, but to look beyond the words. The Spirit showed me that women who are dealing with dry and dead relationships are living in a spiritual Moab or shall I say, "no man's land" just as Ruth had. I couldn't help but take a look at my past relationships and ask myself, had I been in a spiritual Moab? A dry place where there was no life? Did I have to pick up the pieces and walk into a new field that had life and one where a man would notice me? But, what kind of field? How in the world would I get there? And most of all, would I be found by my Boaz?

The Spirit in His patience showed me it was time to stop asking questions, and time to start moving in faith. It was time to leave Moab and journey to a place where not only the Spirit of God resided but my Boaz as well. It was all a matter of being put in position by God and not try to position myself.

Olivia Stith

So I fumbled through the Bible pages and whispered, "Tell the truth Ruth," because a sistah was ready to be found. Boaz was waiting and by God's divine guidance, he would find me.

Journey of Faith I

MOAB FIELDS: NO MAN'S LAND

Olivia Stith

Chapter 1

Leave Them Heathen Ways Alone

"Surely I was sinful at birth, sinful from the time my mother conceived me."
Psalms 51:5-6

Heathen ways are the reason most of us have been or are still caught up in dead relationships. Let me explain. A heathen is one who does things contrary to the way of the living God. Thank God the old saying, "once a heathen always a heathen" is not true. We learn from Ruth that once we allow the Lord to fine tune us, we can learn of his ways and our purpose in life. It's all about being in place.

"In his heart a man plans his course, but the LORD determines his steps."
Proverbs 16:9

In order to get to a new place, we must recognize where we came from so we do not turn back. What are heathen ways? How do they affect the way we choose the men in our lives? We begin to be impacted by heathen ways at birth. It all starts at birth, I tell you! Let's consider a few scenarios of women, single or married, and recognize how heathen ways are seeded into our lives at a very, very young age and goes on to affect us as adults. Now, this does not go for all, because there are always exceptions to life's circumstances.

Many women have been raised in homes without fathers, leaving them to be raised by a single mother or other relatives. Imagine a young daughter seeing her mother work two jobs.

Olivia Stith

Mommy never has time to spend with her family, because she's trying to make ends meet so her family won't starve and Daddy is never around. Mommy comes home after a hard day's work and blurts, "Child you don't need a trifling man to do a thing for you. Get out there and do what you can for yourself. Nobody is going to give you anything!" Now you may think, "Hey that's true. No one is going to do a thing for me, so I have to do it for myself." I'm sure many women have said something like that to or in the presence of our children out of anger, fatigue or frustration of dealing with a man who is not providing as he should. However, look at the words being said and imagine the tone being used when spoken. The seed that has been planted is "you don't need a man." Now the child is left to question if she should trust a man to be responsible and accountable. This is a poisonous seed that takes focus off of the fact that there are good men who will take care of their home and families.

Its effect will be manifested later in the young woman's life. For example, she may develop a dominating spirit that refuses to

submit to the authority of a man as head of the household, because deep inside she believes he will not carry out his duties. She becomes a woman that is driven to get all that she feels she deserves, disregarding the feelings of the man in her life. So the thought that she must be completely self-sufficient is infused by the "you don't need a man" seed. This is how the enemy tricks us into taking up heathen ways. A woman such as this, may find herself in relationships where she is either focusing so much on her career that she has closed off any emotional attachments to a man or has become argumentative and distant because the man feels she has no time for him.

Then there is the woman down the street taking care of business, but the man is lacking ambition and vision to do anything for himself. She doesn't push him because in her eyes she doesn't need him and secondly, she does not love herself enough to insist he go out and become a provider. Again, this is a lifestyle contrary to that which God intended.

Olivia Stith

Some women become so dysfunctional that they allow men to abuse them mentally, physically and/or verbally because it's all they know. They are resistant to sever the relationship because of fear, their children, society, the ministry or a slew of other reasons, thus the heathen seed is spread to a new generation. Others simply dismiss God's order of being with a man altogether and seek to have a relationship with another woman, all tied to the belief that men are trifling. Of course there are many other scenarios. Stay with me as I very quickly show you one more. Consider women who entertain relationships only with men who can give them a certain lifestyle, using their body and wits to obtain all they believe they deserve. Self-preservation and self-satisfaction becomes the idol of the heathen woman living a carefree and reckless life. None of these scenarios is the way God intended for women to behave in relationships.

You can look at another woman's life, like Ruth's, and learn from her experiences. We can compare our own dead, dry relationships to Ruth's native land, Moab or what I refer

to as No Man's Land. Moab was a dry place, a place of unrest and unhappiness. Nothing grew there. Well, I believe Ruth began to tire of her surroundings, and sought a way of escape. If you find yourself in Moab, sooner or later you begin to think to yourself, "There has to be a better way." You began to develop a burning desire in your spirit to leave that place. Sometimes, in our hearts we know the relationship we are in is unhealthy, but we don't know how to get out. This is when we must seek God. He is the only one who can successfully lead you out of Moab. Even though you may not have a relationship with Him yet, your spirit starts to seek Him out. When you seek God, He will be found, then He will direct you on how to get out of a left field relationship and into the right one; you just have to be patient and trusting.

Olivia Stith

Chapter 2

When Church Men Make You Sick: A Mahlon and Chilion Man

"In the days when the judges ruled, there was a famine in the land, and a man from Bethlehem in Judah, together with his wife and two sons, went to live for a while in the country of Moab. The man's name was Elimelech, his wife's name Naomi, and the names of his two sons were Mahlon and Chilion. They were Ephrathites from Bethlehem, Judah. And they went to Moab and lived there."
Ruth 1:1

I'm sure Ruth began to shake her heathen ways when she and her friend, Orpah, met two Jewish brothers who moved to Moab with their family from Bethlehem. The brothers, Mahlon and Chilion were men who knew God, but had other issues. Soon Ruth would learn that Mahlon and Chilion were two sick men!

Their family had left Bethlehem and moved to Moab because of a famine. Imagine that! Men who knew God, moved from the place God inhabited to a nomadic land. Well, it wouldn't make sense for most to leave a so called, "bad situation," to get into something worse, does it? So why would a man with so much power and knowledge come to a place that is dry? Yet the brothers, along with their father, Elimelech, and mother, Naomi, did just that. They left their homeland and established new roots in Moab, thinking the grass was greener on the other side. However, this decision led to disaster. Ultimately, all of the men died and the women were left as grieving widows.

"Now Elimelech, Naomi's husband, died, and she was left with her two sons. They married Moabite women, one named Orpah and the other Ruth. After they had lived there about ten years, both Mahlon and Chilion also died, and Naomi was left without her two sons and her husband." **Ruth 1:3-5**

Olivia Stith

So, let me put you in Ruth's place for a moment. Let's say you enter into a new relationship with a man who knows about God, and he wants to take you from your heathen surroundings. In the process, he introduces you to a God you have never heard of before – the true and living God! And the more you learn of Him, the more your heart yearns to know more.

Suddenly things in your life begin to change. Imagine yourself finally being set free from hanging out and partying in the world. Thanks to this new found love, life is now different and you begin to think you have it made. As you get to know him, you also begin to learn about God and begin seeking Him on a personal level.

The heathen lifestyle and old ways of thinking are put behind you. Yes, you are in a position of newness and this new relationship feels right, but slowly things start to go downhill but... something is not quite right. You begin to feel sick inside as the Lord opens your eyes to a surprising truth. You look around and you're still in Moab.

Why is it that after a while, things that started off good begin to turn for the worse and gradually the well starts to run dry in your relationship? Before long you begin noticing a few things in your new beau that aren't so favorable. You notice weaknesses in him that that are not desirable or Christian-like. For example, he may want to caress or become intimate with you before the appointed time. He may try to control you by his words, as though he is superior to you. He may even attempt to spiritually manipulate you because he was the one who introduced you to the Lord. Believe me, it happens. Some men fail to remember its God who saved you and not them! You need to know that none of these behaviors are healthy.

You see, these actions are similar to the heathen men of our past. "But, at least he's a Christian," you may think to yourself.

Olivia Stith

He may have the knowledge and be able to talk about God to you, but he is not effective and you will need to step back from any man who professes to be a child of God, but displays the same behaviors as those in the world. When you have a desire to change your life and move out of sinful relationships, the enemy knows this as well. So he just changes the scheme. He makes things look a little sweeter, but he still has the ultimate plan, which is to leave you alone and withered in the spirit.

This is why many women are hurt and shocked when they meet a man who claims he loves the Lord, but after a while shows that his spirit is sin sick. They have connected with a man who has lost his place with God and moved from His presence. What catches us off guard with this kind of man is that he knows how to do "religious" things like quote scripture, shout 'til his shoes come off and all that jazz. We mistake that his actions are as one who has a relationship with God, but all that whooping and hollering, doesn't prove a thing. Many can act the part, but none can live the life unless the Spirit resides in them.

"He is the kind who worms his way into the home of a weak-willed woman and gains control. He is loaded down with sin and swayed by all kinds of evil desires, always learning but never able to acknowledge the truth."
2 Timothy 3:1-7

You'd better watch out sistah! This man is sick in the head. He feels like he can live a life as a child of God, in a place that God does not reside. This means a place out of His order and away from Him; a place that he cannot hear the voice of God or be in position to respond when God does move. He may speak of God but he has no power to operate in the ways of God. This leads to a trap that the enemy pulls this man into - and if you are not careful, you will allow his problems to weigh on your spirit and he will take you down with him. Eventually his spiritual life will fade to be one of sin and he will end up dying in the world.

Now you see why you don't want a Mahlon and Chilion man? Their names even mean weak and sickly. That tells you something

Olivia Stith

right there. Honey, one thing is for sure, a man will live up to his name or die trying!

"Those who live according to the sinful nature have their minds set on what that nature desires; but those who live in accordance with the Spirit have their minds set on what the Spirit desires. The mind of sinful man is death, but the mind controlled by the Spirit is life and peace; the sinful mind is hostile to God. It does not submit to God's law, nor can it do so. Those controlled by the sinful nature cannot please God."
Romans 5:5-8

Another thing to keep in mind, if you are in a relationship, note some key behaviors of your man. You never want to be tied to man who claims he loves the Lord, but at the first sign of trouble he picks up and run. When the bills get behind or the job gets stressful how does he handle it? Does he trust that God will provide? If a man does not have faith, he will run to whatever will make his life easier. Does his attitude change when people irritate him? Be wise to recognize important signs and not jeopardize your

relationship with God because of a relationship with a man. Now if you find that you are already tangled up in a not so pleasant relationship with a church man who has truly shown you that he is no different than the men in the world, (with the exception of knowing a few scriptures) - don't be dismayed. With this newly acquired knowledge, you are not destined to stay in a dry place. You need to rejoice in the Lord when these relationships die! God has set you free. Take the good from the bad and move on.

Remember, that even in these hurtful relationships, all things are working for your good, because, you have connected with the One who can guide you even in the midst of your problems, Jesus Christ. Broken relationships should make you draw closer to him; He still has a plan for your happiness. You can't help what another man does, but you can be in control of your next move. The average woman may become frustrated and wants to give up on finding a decent man. She is thinking there aren't any good men out there in the world and the

Olivia Stith

ones in church are just as bad. That's a normal reaction, but there is more to think about. This is the time to focus on your relationship with Christ. Focus on the positive that came out of these types of relationships and not the negative. All life experiences have lessons to be learned. God is just positioning you in place and taking you to a new field of thinking. He will lead you into your divine purpose and the divine connection you seek.

Now the true shift is ready to take place. You have had a taste of God, and your spirit desires more. You soon realize there are many other women out there like you. Even though you may be ready to step forward, realize every woman does not have the wisdom to move ahead when she has been broken so many times. You will be surprised why.

Chapter 3

All Sisters Can't Roll with You: Leaving Moab - No Man Land

"When she heard in Moab that the LORD had come to the aid of his people by providing food for them, Naomi and her daughters-in-law prepared to return home from there. With her two daughters-in-law she left the place where she had been living and set out on the road that would take them back to the land of Judah."
Ruth 1:6

When their husbands died, Naomi, Ruth and Orpah had decisions to make. They could either stay where they were or move on to another place. The men that held them in Moab were no longer alive. Isn't it amazing how the very thing holding you down, the Lord disposes of so you can be set free?

Olivia Stith

Set free so that you can receive direction from him, which was just how these ladies found themselves – needing direction for a journey. Suddenly it was just them and God. Follow me as I bring this same situation into our times.

You may not realize it, but the friends and people in your life are a part of your journey. You will deal with your own Orpahs and Naomis who will be a vital part of you getting into place in order to meet the one God has destined for you. Naomi heard that Bethlehem was no longer in a famine and knowing that staying in Moab served no purpose, she decided to journey back to where she had come.

That's just like God to allow us to return to His open arms after we have distanced ourselves from him. Well Naomi was returning home, but sadly, she felt that she could no longer be of any help to the Ruth and Orpah so when they followed her, she begged them to return to their own families in Moab.

"With her two daughters-in-law she left the place where she had been living and set out on the road that would take them back to the land of Judah. Then Naomi said to her two daughters-in-law; Go back, each of you, to your mother's home. May the LORD show kindness to you, as you have shown to your dead and to me. May the LORD grant that each of you will find rest in the home of another husband."
Ruth 1:7-9

Orpah, after much pondering, decided she would return to her people. You would think a woman who had been introduced to God would not make a choice such as that. Your Orpah-type friends will show much of the same personality traits that Orpah had. They will walk only so far with you and then turn back. It's heartbreaking when you see the cares of life causing those you care for to return to a lifestyle that God has delivered them from, but don't let this stop you. It is no longer about friends and family dictating what's best for your life.

Olivia Stith

Don't be surprised if it happens to be the very sisters who you have worked side by side with in serving the Lord. The reason being, after seeing how fickle some men can be, their overall mindsets are stuck into thinking "all men are the same," which is bred by hurt and pain. Their minds are poisoned with carnal thinking, so they turn back to their heathen ways. A disturbing truth is the only reason many of them stayed in a union with Christ is because the man who they were tied to was in the faith.

When Orpah's husband died, her faith died with him. Your faith in God should not be based on and rooted in a man's faith, but your own. If you're serving God because of your relationship with a man it will never work. God is looking for a sincere relationship with you, not one based on the conditions of someone being in your life. The Lord requires us to have Him first in our lives and man second. No one should ever come before Him, whether they introduced you to Him or not.

Remember, that person did not save your soul, God did! It's no longer about being with a man, but surviving and building a life for you. Keep in mind that during difficult times of your life you may not get the support and words of encouragement from these women, because they are operating in the flesh and not the spirit.

"Return home, my daughters; I am too old to have another husband. Even if I thought there was still hope for me - even if I had a husband tonight and then gave birth to sons- would you wait until they grew up? Would you remain unmarried for them? No, my daughters. It is more bitter for me than for you, because the LORD's hand has gone out against me!" At this they wept again. Then Orpah kissed her mother-in-law good-by, but Ruth clung to her."
Ruth 1:12-14

Olivia Stith

Chapter 4

Old Wives Tell No Tales: Connecting to Your Naomi

Now, in Naomi's situation, she was a woman who truly knew God. Even so, during her season of grief in Moab, she didn't have the best advice for her daughter-in-laws. Naomi knew that God was providing in Bethlehem and there was only death was in Moab. In her heart she knew she had to leave, but by her being in Moab for so long, her thinking had been affected as well. So this is why her advice was not wise. There will be a time when even the wisest woman of God may not necessarily be in a position to give you good advice. Not that she is intentionally trying to lead you the wrong way, but in the midst of her own suffering, she is trying to save you from going through the same hardships. But through that, the enemy attempted to play a trick on Ruth. He knew that her destiny was tied to Naomi and if Ruth stayed in Moab her purpose would never be fulfilled. The devil tries this strategy all the time. This is why we have to be discerning and knowledgeable even in talking to women of God who have contended in the faith, but are going through trials and tribulations. She may advise out of her temporal situation rather than allowing herself to be led by the Spirit in the advice she gives. Emotion-based advice rather than counsel based upon the word of God is not wisdom. Take heed that advice given based solely on one's feelings may cause another to be out of place with God. If Ruth had followed Naomi's advice, imagine how many lives would have been impacted. Divine wisdom and knowledge is what it takes to get us from one field of mind to another.

"Know also that wisdom is sweet to your soul; if you find it, there is a future hope for you, and your hope will not be cut off."
Proverbs 24:14

Olivia Stith

Ruth also had to decide whether to stay with her friend in a land she had known all her life as home, or to go against the wishes of Naomi and head to a foreign land. She had to choose between staying in an old place or moving into new territory. It is time to set aside the advice of the Orpah-type sisters and focus on the ones who are moving ahead and not backwards. Seek the face of God for yourself.

My friend, please know that it is not up to anyone to decide what God will bring you to or take you through. The key thing is that if God has brought it into your life, He is able to take you through it. Know that our God is merciful and He moves and reaches us even in the driest places such as Moab. One thing you must realize is that in pain it's so much easier to just sit in a rut and not press forward into the unknown. The mind fights against treading into the unknown when it's already suffered heartache. The fear you hold on to is that life may get worse, and you just can't take any more pain.

But God gives us the drive to press forward through the pain. Ruth chose to leave Moab for Bethlehem. God's plan prevailed, for He still used Naomi's being out of position to put Ruth in her rightful position. Ruth was beginning to move into her destiny by forsaking all she'd trusted before, and instead trusting God.

For some women, going back is comfortable because the territory is familiar, which is always easier than heading to a place that requires faith. But why would you want to wander again into a place or a relationship that you know God has no part of? You should not allow anyone, not your mother, sister nor brother, to talk you into going back to the way of life you left behind. There is no turning back! Do not go back into the sinful relationships regardless what others around you choose. The love of a man may have pulled you out of place with God, but He is able to restore you and put you back in position, if you press forward without looking back.

Olivia Stith

"Brethren, I count not myself to have apprehended: but this one thing I do, forgetting those things which are behind, and reaching forth unto those things, which are before."
Philippians 3: 13

God requires us to trust him and have faith when man has failed us. By trusting in Him you believe He will reward you. Even though you may not understand all that is happening in your life, you need to thank him for this season in your life. For in this season you're at the place that He is your lover and guide, and will lead and direct you in all truths. Not everyone will not fight the good fight of faith, but my friend, you have to forsake it all and move forward believing that God has already set the path ahead. You must do this through prayer and supplication.

"The Lord is near. Do not be anxious about anything, but in everything, by prayer and petition, with thanksgiving, present your requests to God. And the peace of God, which transcends all understanding, will guard your hearts and your minds in Christ

Jesus."
Philippians 4:5-7

Now is the time to regroup your way of thinking, renew your mind and forsake the past. Believe that even though you feel you're going through a spiritual death because of the hurt, God is able to restore you. All of it may be foreign to you, and you can't see how things will turn out, but be strong and keep the faith. Know that God will never leave nor forsake you. Pick up your heart and head to your Bethlehem. There is nothing left in Moab! God has released you to greener fields. Don't worry about who is going with you. Just pick up the pieces of your life and keep pressing forward. You may not realize it, but it's all in God's plan to get you in the right field. It's time to leave "no man land."

So even though Naomi didn't have the wisest advice for her daughter-in-laws, was there anything that Ruth could learn from Naomi? Yes! Again Naomi was key in getting Ruth to her Destiny. Have you taken time to sit amongst women of wisdom and

Olivia Stith

seek direction on how to move forward in different areas of your life?

Do you trust that God has input knowledge in others so you can get on the right path? One of the most important things that led Ruth to Boaz that most do not realize was her heart.

Not in the aspect of it loving him, because she had not met him yet, but her heart of forsaking herself for the love of her mother-in-law. So don't miss out on receiving wisdom from women of God who can direct your steps in where God wants to use you. Pray that God sets women before you that can be trusted and are active in the increasing of the kingdom. I'm not speaking on a woman of questionable character, but instead I'm talking about a godly woman, even though she may be going through tough times. The reason she can offer guidance is that she speaks wisdom, based not only on her life's experiences, but the word of God. If the advice is based on kingdom teaching, it doesn't matter what situation the person is in, it is God's word that is going to move in your life.

"Likewise, teach the older women to be reverent in the way they live, not to be slanderers or addicted to much wine, but to teach what is good. Then they can train the younger women to love their husbands and children, to be self-controlled and pure, to be busy at home, to be kind, and to be subject to their husbands, so that no one will malign the word of God."
Titus 2:3-6

Stay connected to your Naomis! You see Naomi in the midst of all that she lost, never lost faith in God. This is why Ruth kept moving forward in love, because surrounding yourself with people who don't give up in the midst of adversity, strengthens and encourages you. It may not necessarily always be a woman, but even men of God. The recognizable trait in this person is they know how to give you instruction and keep you focused. They know the steps to get to a place where God resides. Life may be giving them bumps and bruises, but if you step forward and embrace them while you all are journeying together, you become helpers, one of the other. You see, any time a person

Olivia Stith

is imparting something in your life that brings life and moving with it, you know it's productive. So take a moment to appreciate those who counsel you and serve as a beacon of light.

Now here is another key to all of this. Your love for God will have to come first before you can have a love for man. As long as you're in a relationship with God, the natural man will come into place. He must always be first because this love will show you how to act towards others. Why is this? Because your heart has now been conditioned to know that life is about serving others and not only yourself. Your purpose cannot be solely on getting what is best for you; it has to be about others. You will realize that in helping others you're really helping yourself move from one level to another. Is this not the case with Ruth? Once she and Naomi transitioned to Bethlehem, she continued to dwell with, support and serve her mother-in-law.

Even though it may not seem logical in our minds, our love and service to others will lead us to his path. Our connections with people who have been to places in the spirit and natural are what we need. There is not a person on this earth that knows it all, or can make it on his or her own without any help. We all have a purpose in the lives of those around us. Recognize what that is for the people in your life. You can't separate the events of your life from your meeting the right person because it takes all of your life and affects that divine meeting in the end. Don't be afraid to serve, and do your part to be a blessing to others. Your work will not go unnoticed, even though it may seem in the beginning that you're doing a little part. God has big plans for you because of your sacrifice.

So ask yourself, are you ready to take your mind off the man and focus on serving the Lord? You may not realize it, but this is what God is after, a woman that is willing to work in the vineyard not because she is expecting something, but because of her love for Him and others. This love for the Lord will be the light that will bring Boaz your way. You best believe that... Just ask Ruth!

Olivia Stith

Journey of Faith II

BETHLEHEM FIELDS: WORKING FOR BOAZ

Chapter 5

You Gotta Work It Sister and Get the Field of Things

Finally you have made it to Bethlehem! Life is grand and everything is going to go as planned right? Well not so fast! There is work to be done. In fact, when most women reach Bethlehem, it's because they have reached the end of their road in relationships and are just seeking relief. They have lost everything and many times in their heart they have given up on love. At least most think that way. Now, when the two women arrived in Bethlehem a harvest was going on in the land. God was providing for His people.

"So Naomi returned from Moab ccompanied by Ruth the Moabitess, her daughter-in-law, arriving in Bethlehem as the barley harvest was beginning."
Ruth 1:22

Olivia Stith

The mindset of Naomi when she entered the city and was greeted by her friends, echoes the thoughts of many sisters today...

"Don't call me Naomi," she told them. "Call me Mara, because the Almighty has made my life very bitter. I went away full, but the LORD has brought me back empty. Why call me Naomi? The LORD has afflicted me; the Almighty has brought misfortune upon me."
Ruth 1:20-21

Doesn't that sound like some of us at a certain point? Things are always in order when we abide in our Bethlehem, because this is the place where God resides. However, as soon as we move from his presence into Moab, life will become bitter. It's hard and we only experience the death of things, for in Him is life, our lives, our dreams and our love. But, now as Naomi said, she came back empty with nothing. Once again this is how the carnal mind wants to see things.

Even when you get to Bethlehem the pain will still be there, and the enemy will want you to think you have lost it all but we know God has many unseen plans. Sometimes it's His will, believe it or not, to be empty. When we are empty inside, God is able to pour into our spirits and refresh us. We can be renewed and restored.

In order to be cleansed from the sinful Moab fields, our minds have to be changed. We have to be restored to know that regardless of what it looks like, God is still able to keep His promise. He just wants us to get back in position and to be in His service in the Bethlehem fields.Remember it takes work though. It takes work in a field that will yield you a harvest and in that field lays the path to Boaz. Now that's enough to keep us going, right? Keep this in mind while you are out there working. So often you will hear people stating that there is a man shortage and few good men out there, but I beg to differ. God has put you in a kingdom field to reap the blessings He has for you. This includes a mate as well. How can there be a shortage in the place that is having

Olivia Stith

a harvest? Is God not able to have a man for you, your sister, your mother and whoever desires to work in His vineyard? It is time to stop basing your future on the world's statistics. Put your faith and trust in God.

"It is better to trust in the LORD than to put confidence in man."
Psalms 118:8

He is the creator of the world and from the beginning of time, He destined that man and woman should be together.

God is still on the throne and he has someone for you so be strong and don't lose heart. It may look dim, but God works behind the scenes. He has a plan for you, and you may not realize it. In fact, as I said, this is the point where your focus is on what you have to do in the kingdom fields, by helping others and serving the Lord. The only way you will be found is if you get in the fields and start working.

What do I mean by working in the fields? Working and serving God in all areas of your life including your family, friends, dreams and aspirations. You should seek God's face about what to do, when to do it, and with whom to do it so that you can reap the fruits of your labor. Once He shows you, get to work! God must see that you will be a faithful worker to Him "first" before you are released to a man. This is the time that the world will notice that even though you're alone, you are a woman of substance. The fields are doing things in the world through godly standards to reap benefits for the kingdom. As you know you have to keep things flowing and growing by the living water or you will wither and die in certain areas of your life. You definitely don't want that to happen!

If you don't get out there and focus on the things of life that has been set forth for you, your spirit will starve.

Olivia Stith

You don't have time to mope in a place where God resides, because in Him comes your comfort. You can't focus on your ministry, your children, or your mind when you're sitting around crying. Weeds and all kinds of things will start growing in your field. It's time to put your hand to the plow and start flowing in the spirit. Do it with diligence, not because it's what you think God wants, but rather what you want to do for God. This is where the blessings lie.

"We, however, will not boast beyond proper limits, but will confine our boasting to the field God has assigned to us, a field that reaches even to you."
2 Corinthians 10:13

Know that the work you're doing in the kingdom is not only going to benefit you, but all the souls that God has placed in your life. You cannot sit and wait around for a man to come in your life and take care of you and your needs.

You must work while it's day. Work has to be done whether you are in a relationship or not. There is no other way around it. You can do it, because if God has set it before you, you possess the abilities to get it done. Inside of you dwells gifts and abilities that you may have never dreamed of until you are put in a position to use them. In fact the people and places your life walk takes you on, may seem foreign to you, but God has put you in each place for a reason.

"Direct me in the path of your commands, for there I find delight." **Psalms 119:35**

Ruth was a foreigner in Bethlehem. She took the initiative and the low seat, as a gleaner in the fields, praying that anyone would find favor on her in her work. At the moment she did not know that the very field she was gleaning in was a step towards her destiny and was ready to unfold.

Olivia Stith

We know the favor of God was on her life and in return He would give her favor in the eyes of Boaz.

That's how God operates in your life. Things may look foreign to you and you may not even be used to doing things a certain way, but a new way of living in Christ brings on a new lifestyle. This is when your trust in God strengthens. You're in a foreign place but you know it's the right place. Ruth knew this.

You may think you're out doing ministry, being a good steward over your home, living holy, helping those in need and yet no one sees it. In fact, you may not have the big title or fancy job, but you're doing the best you can. Or maybe you do have a big job and title, but you are humble and take the low seat. You have favor with God , and he will give you favor with that man of God.

"May the favor of the Lord our God rest upon us; establish the work of our hands for us - yes, establish the work of our hands."
Psalms 90:17

This is the thing about your season; you may even not know that you're in it! Oh, but you do know that you're in Bethlehem because you are in the presence of God and life is flowing. You just don't know that you are in the spiritual field that God has set up for Boaz to find you. God does this for a reason, its called focus.

He wants you to focus on what is most important right now. Focus not just on things that He has to instill in you, but also on the things that He has to do to establish your character with those around you. Trust me; God will not have you just out there working for nothing. There are benefits and He will ensure your name speaks for itself. Your name, meaning your character, is who you are as a person.

Character is so important in all aspects of our life, especially being single and out there in the world. Remember, Ruth was outside of Bethlehem in a field which we know spiritually represents the world.

Olivia Stith

So when you are out in the world doing work for the kingdom, what will be spoken of your character? Will you be known as a busy body that spreads gossip or a woman of a few words? Are you a woman that shows personality and class or are you worldly or overly preachy? You should not be cold hearted and unapproachable. Think about the way you communicate with people around you. What would they say of your conversation behind closed doors? Would your church members testify that you are a woman who puts her hands to the plow and finish projects? These are important things to remember in your judgment of being worthy as wife material. All in all, it's your character sister.

A name speaks for itself. What better name can be established than the name that God gives you before men?. It's time to make a name for yourself , so when God lays your name on that man's heart, you will answer. Honey, when God is finished setting things up, you will be sitting back in awe.

Chapter 6

Make Sure You Get the Right Field of Things!

"So she went out and began to glean in the fields behind the harvesters. As it turned out, she found herself working in a field belonging to Boaz, who was from the clan of Elimelech."
Ruth 2:3

Ruth unknowingly began to work in a field owned by Boaz; she had no idea God was setting her up for a life change. Isn't that just like God, doing things in the unseen? Putting us in a foreign place, but the entire time building up our familiarity? When you first step into Boaz's field or path you will most likely not even be aware of it, because the actual field is not in Bethlehem. Sounds strange right? Boaz first saw Ruth on the outside.

Olivia Stith

"Just then Boaz arrived from Bethlehem and greeted the harvesters, "The LORD be with you!"
Ruth 2:4

I know you are thinking, "What, after all this and I'm still not inside Bethlehem?" Spiritually you are in Bethlehem, God's presence, but the work is on the outside in the world. We just have to make sure that when we're in that field outside of Bethlehem, it is the right one. Your works will let you know which one you're in. Are you bearing fruit in your work? Or are things dying around you without any sense of hope? Moab is the field of no hope. You live in the body of Christ, which is Bethlehem and work in His fields, ministry, church and such. Okay, but check this out... This particular field, which is the world with lost souls, is outside of Bethlehem. Sinners are outside of the body of Christ, but it is up to us to harvest souls and bring them in. It's all part of the process and hard work. Don't get me wrong; you're reaping not only in the kingdom but in this world as well. So when you bring souls from the world, you're bringing a harvest back into Bethlehem, which is the body of Christ.

"Let us not become weary in doing good, for at the proper time we will reap a harvest if we do not give up."
Galatians 6:9

Back to the fields outside of Bethlehem... If you are doing kingdom work then you are working this part of the field as well, because this is the section where you are working for souls that are weak and open to receive the word of the Lord. This field is not in the actual body of Christ, but as you work it, you bring the souls into it. Let me say it plain and clear. God's purpose for us is to win souls for the kingdom.

Your ministry and your fellow brothers in Christ are key factors in this vineyard that your Boaz will find you in, because the seeds that other children of God plant are the ones that will require you to go and harvest and bring back to the body of Christ.

Olivia Stith

"I planted the seed, Apollos watered it, but God made it grow."
1 Corinthians 3:6

Through these actions Boaz will see you while you are out there working in the fields. In this section is where he will take notice of you. Now we know the fields of the world are big, so how in the world will you know where to be positioned? News flash, you won't know! It's not for you to know remember? This is why, you must stay focused on doing the work God has for you and move in places as He guides you. Whether its part of ministry, a job, or whatever that may be foreign to you, you will know that it is Him pulling on your heart to do it. There is a reason. These fields are big and you must be placed in the right spot to be found. So it's not about sitting in church waiting on a man, you must get outside the walls and be found.

Boaz is part of the body of Christ, but he still oversees the workers by making sure they are taken care of as well as doing a good work.

So naturally when a man sees a new worker, "you" out there, he will take notice! It's going to be something about you that catches his attention and when it does, "all eyes are on you." It's time to find out from his fellow workers and friends, who's that girl? Alright now, it has already begun! Let's keep moving to the next phase because finally you have been seen!

Olivia Stith

Chapter 7

Man-n-n….Who is that Girl!!! What is her Name?

Once you step forth and start working the path God has for you, a lot of eyes will be on you. When Boaz came to the fields, he noticed a new face in the crowd. "Boaz asked the foreman of his harvesters, "Whose young woman is that?" It was Ruth! Alright, here it is, yes! Boaz notices Ruth, but inquires of her with his trusted worker. Oh I love it! Ruth catches his eye and he asks, "Do you know if she has a husband?" Here is a man getting the facts before he even proceeds to make any contact with a woman. Why is he doing it? Simply because he is ensuring sure he is not treading on some other man's wife or lady friend. There goes that integrity. A real man is going to speak to someone who can offer the truth and wisdom before he steps to a woman of God. Boaz is not just talking to anyone, but the overseer of his land.

This shows that there was trust between the two men. Boaz obviously trusted the man's judgment and assessment of people. It's like most men, you know, they have their boys' back. Yes, they're going to tell all they know.

Now watch out girlfriend, sounds like a character check getting ready to happen. Your Boaz could be behind the scenes inquiring about you and you don't even know it! A noble woman does not have to worry about what will be said. Her works will speak for her. Her focus is not on being part of the crowd but doing what God has purposed in her life. This includes her career, ministry, family and such. She walks through life determined to embrace all the Lord has promised her.

This is a praying and fasting sister, because she knows in her flesh she cannot become a woman of virtue without the Lord on her side. A man is looking for this kind of woman, because she will have his back in the good and bad times.

Olivia Stith

She can be trusted to handle his business naturally and spiritually; the sister can work it and still remain virtuous. She is a woman that he does not have to worry about bringing around his friends and family. Oh, we know some folks you can't bring home to mama! He enjoys her company, because this woman doesn't have time to play games with a Moab mentality! Becoming a woman such as this requires time alone with God; time to allow him to mold you into whom you are to become. It requires a season of being alone to get things in perspective.

The result of that necessary alone time is the sister walking around complete in her way of thinking and doing her thing. She has been through the transition. She will stand out in the crowd, because she is focusing on what's going on in her life and not concerned about what everyone else is doing or what they think. Remember, she is operating in the world, but she is not of the world. This woman stands alone.

A name is so important and once you imprint it on the hearts of people they will never forget who you are. Your name and credibility will be spoken of by someone, whether you know it or not. It may be after the man meets you, but someone is calling your name; be careful what name you choose to answer to.

Now after he asks his boys about you, he's definitely going to God ask about you!

A man of God will do this if he is wise, because he wants to know what he will be dealing with. Boaz may be inquiring about you without your knowledge, and God does this for a reason. Now let's be honest here, if God secretly shared with you the identity of your mate, wouldn't your behavior and thoughts change just because you knew? You would become more cautious about how you carried yourself or the friends you spent time with. I'm sure you would make an effort to be in the same circles as that man. Let's keep it real. Honey your eyes would be on him all the time!

Olivia Stith

Oh and don't let another woman come near him...it would be on! You see, we all are human and it's our natural instinct to be protective of what is ours. Imagine us having that knowledge, changing things and worst of all trying to advise God! So the Lord in all His majesty allows things to happen on a course where we may not see it but He is working behind the scenes. Just like with Ruth! Yes that's right, you may not know it.

Your mama may not know it, Aunt Lucy may not know it, but believe me someone does. You may not know it, but sister in this season you'll be spotted by Boaz!

Now do you think a man is going to be drawn to a sister tied to church drama or one who he hears is always jumping from one brother to the next? Lord forbid if he hears about one who is always sleeping around...

You know what I mean? The strange and sad thing about it is most women will not sit still and allow God to mold them into the type of woman a man is looking for. They lack the patience in waiting on the Lord and instead run ahead of Him. Consequently, they only have half of the qualities needed to be complete for a man. Many of them get half way healed and then quickly jump back into the dating field. Why? Why move when you are only half way done? Half will not do it; the same way ninety-nine will not do, you should always strive for one hundred percent.

When it's known that you aren't hanging out doing things of the world or running around with foolish women who have no standards or goals in life, you are making a name for yourself. You will be the same as Ruth, in the midst of a field of women, but you will stand out. Girl, if you didn't know, now you do! So work on building a good name for yourself because behind the scenes inquiring minds, or shall I say a brother is going to say: Man-n-n…who is that girl?

Chapter 8

Oh to be Young at Heart and Old in Spirit

We now know character is important when the mind of the man of God becomes inquisitive and starts churning. Remember what Boaz did:

"Boaz asked the foreman of his harvesters, "Whose young woman is that?"
Ruth 2:5

There was something about Ruth that caught his eye besides being the new girl in the field. He noticed her beauty amongst the hot heat and dirt. Regardless of all the gleaning she was doing, picking up left over sheaves, she had youthful glow illuminating from her spirit. An innocence I would say... This truly drew Boaz who was much older than Ruth. I know you're thinking, "An older man is drawn to a younger woman?"

Let's look at this a little bit deeper. So we're not speaking old in terms of age, but old as in maturity in life and the spirit.

Well, let's look at the terms old and young pertaining to a man and a woman. A man old in the spirit let's say represents someone who is seasoned in the Spirit. You see, your Boaz may not be naturally old but old can represent being seasoned. He has lived life and learned from the experiences. He knows how to battle in the spiritual sense. He is knowledgeable of the ways of the Lord and has been living them for a long time. Now of course this can apply to a woman too, but let's focus on the concept behind Boaz being "older." You want a man who is old in the spirit. You do not want some inexperienced man who has never been through anything in life.

A man who is, as the old folks say - still wet behind the ears. This man has to be able to handle challenges on a mature level, know how to be a role model, know how to be that husband and the head of his home.

Olivia Stith

A man who won't just jump up and do things without considering the cost or the impact it will have on his family. Don't you feel safe knowing God has been working in a man's life and he's not some sporadic "jump up and do it today, lay it down tomorrow" type of man? This brother has learned that life is not just about him, but the lives of others around him are also important.

Imagine dealing with a man who is not going to play with your feelings, because the heart of God is moving his emotions. You don't have to worry about this man putting you in uncompromising situations, especially if he has respect for you as a woman of God. Emotions may rise and the heart may flutter with desire, but he is not recklessness with his mind or body. He is not concerned with jumping between the sheets ahead of time, but would rather wait on things to happen in due season.

Because he's spent time with God he knows that a spur of the moment thrill cannot guarantee a life of happiness when it is rooted from sin. Do you think just any man could respect you to this degree? Most definitely not! It takes one who worships, honors and is living a life of obedience to God that will know how to treat you in the same manner. This is not the behavior of some babe in Christ. This all comes with age or maturity, am I right? So think on this... you want a man who is old in the spirit and walks by the Spirit, Amen!

"For those who live according to the flesh set their minds on the things of the flesh, but those who live according to the Spirit, the things of the Spirit."
Romans 8:5

And you know what? He will be looking for a young woman! Now, before my older sisters start tearing pages and the younger ones start throwing high fives, let me explain. Remember, we're speaking in the spirit with this Ruth and Boaz experience. Some of the attributes of being young in

Olivia Stith

heart are purity, submissiveness, humbleness, and trustworthiness. A young hearted woman follows Christ because He is the head authoritarian in her life.

This is why this type of sister glows with youthfulness in the midst of the storms or heat of life fields. She's independent, yet humble enough to lean and depend on her husband. Remember, her heart belongs first to Christ who has shown her real love. Now that she knows what it is and how it feels, she knows God will lead her to the path of that special one.

When God moves a woman's heart; she will see changes in both her life and relationships. Even though most men may appear hard nosed on the outside, a man wants a woman who is feminine, strong and compassionate. Now I know you're saying, "I want a compassionate man too," of course you do, but let's keep looking at this from a man's perspective. For one thing, all women are not compassionate, strong or feminine. It seems some of us are stuck in that Moab "Orpah still hurt - so I'm staying in the past mode," with hardened hearts. It's hard to show compassion when you feel it has not been shown to you. Now many get attributes such as compassion, femininity and oh yes, please don't let me forget humbleness, confused with weakness but a Godly woman can be compassionate, feminine and humble, and strong at the same time. She can be young in spirit and still bold.

Ruth also had a humble and caring heart that operated with compassion, shown in her love for her mother in law, which would catch Boaz's attention. So yes, just as Boaz was looking at young Ruth in the field and gaining more insight about her, someone just maybe watching you. So keep glowing! Even in the midst of your going through the rough and dusty trials, this brother sees your beauty. Life ups and downs should not take that youthful glow from your face on the outside as long as the Spirit of God abiding and renewing you from the outside. Speak it! You are young and renewed, just as Ruth was becoming! All you need to know is that God is behind the scenes working this divine plan out.

Olivia Stith

A godly man is drawn to a woman out there saying, "Yes, I'm handling my Fathers business in the fields, but I am still a woman with passion and femininity underneath all of this." You are saying inside, "I'm open to being taken care of and giving my heart to you." In fact, we want to scream that loudly many times. Trust me, a man can hear you and the right one will come, because men of God are looking for a new thing. A new thing that's different from the old women of the past, those Moab types. They want this breath of fresh air - you, who stands out from the crowds. They want you, a foreigner to this world, but not in the eyes of your Boaz because you are both in the body of Christ.

Chapter 9

Girl Folks Been Talking

Just in case you don't know, people talk. People watch you daily and then go on to talk about you. Sometimes it's good, other times it's not. What they say may be the truth or a lie; but either way they talk. So the key thing is, don't give them anything to talk about. If they do speak negatively based on false information, it's on them and not you.

You can't control what comes out of other people's mouths, but you surely can control how you allow it to effect you. How you act towards people will be known to others, so be very careful how you entertain people you don't know.

You may be sitting next to someone in a restaurant, or at the beauty shop that has ties to a man who is admiring you from afar.

Olivia Stith

This is why carrying yourself as a woman of integrity and character is so important. Your life will be your testament to someone behind closed doors. Who you are will reflect who is drawn to you. Look at how Ruth's life opened the door for her meeting Boaz through her contact with the foreman.

"The foreman replied, "She is the Moabitess who came back from Moab with Naomi."
Ruth 2:6

This aroused Boaz curiosity the more, because he knew Naomi was a widow and had lost her sons. Why would a woman from a foreign land come with her and labour amongst strangers? Imagine, most people would think the odds are against a woman coming from a heathen land versus those who were believers in God, but it was not. Why is this? It's simple... She used to live in Moab but she came back with Naomi. Yes, you may have lived in the world, in Moab, but you have been called out of the world.

"So from now on we regard no one from a worldly point of view. Though we once regarded Christ in this way, we do so no longer. Therefore, if anyone is in Christ, he is a new creation; the old has gone, the new has come."
2 Corinthians 5:16-17

People see those you associate with, especially those who are reputable and have a good name. We know from the beginning, when Naomi came back to Bethlehem, that people were glad to see her again. This woman was well respected and not only that, she was tied to Boaz. Don't you think Boaz knew Naomi's character?

This will be similar to that man of God who will be interested in you. I'm sure he knows a few people who you associate with. You just never know who and how close he is with any of them.

Olivia Stith

Let it be known that those in your circle are women and men who are movers and shakers in this world, not idle gossipers and drama queens. It shows that you are wise in who you allow in your world. Remember, your friends and associates will become his and a man will be mindful of these things. He will be watching to see if you hang with the women who always cause drama, you know, the ones who sit around doing nothing with their life. He will definitely get the 411 on you. Girl, you best believe it!

One thing I want to definitely stress is this.It does not matter where you came from or what type of life you used to live, that's irrelevant. What matters now is that you are living a new life that is set aside from the old. So don't allow the enemy to make you feel that your past will cause you to be passed over by a good man. You are a new creature in Christ Jesus and you will be with a man who has a new mindset. A mindset that is guided by the Spirit and not what he thinks he knows.

He doesn't judge you from the past. He knows that God is able to change all people, even him!

He remembers that, we all were sinners, so have confidence that regardless of where God has brought you from, He is able to get you to the place He has destined for you. You came this far right? The Lord has brought you from where you were for a reason and placed you in position for a reason. The least amongst people of God will exalt to the greatest. The last shall truly be the first! So honey, trust me, its not about who has the best dress, the socioeconomic status, the highest position or the strongest anointing. Sister, it's about whom God has placed in position to be found and that can deliver His will. Be content and confident that God will allow you to be found. When God puts you in the fields where Boaz will find you, He is divinely setting it up so that you stand out. Don't be moved by the crowds but simply be moved by the Spirit of God.

Olivia Stith

You must keep that spirit of humbleness as Ruth did and you will give someone great things to say about you without even trying. Does it matter if you leading the choir, or have a high profile job at the moment? What's important to you? Is it being seen or is it being content in what God has for you? Do you see how every decision you make will influence how people see you? It should not matter if you are in the forefront or in the background. The only eyes you want to stay in front of are God's! If you do this, the other things that you need and desire will be given to you willingly. The Lord honors a humble heart and spirit that is not concerned about being seen but rather doing the work of the kingdom.

"Your beginnings will seem humble, so prosperous will your future be."
Job 8:7

Remember God must first know that you are serious about working in His vineyard before He trusts you with one of His sons! How many of us would take a lowly position of picking up leftovers to live like Ruth? She didn't even get the full wheat; she got the leftovers yet the sister still worked diligently.

"She went into the field and has worked steadily from morning till now, except for a short rest in the shelter."
Ruth 2:7

This is not the time to be hanging around and waiting on things to happen. Its time to get on the grind while knowing your works will speak for you! You are working on life rewards for this side and the one to come. It's not easy and at times may be risky, but there's nothing like a woman who displays boldness and assertiveness but has no qualms about taking the back seat.

Olivia Stith

"All of you, clothe yourselves with humility toward one another, because, God opposes the proud but gives grace to the humble. Humble yourselves, therefore, under God's mighty hand, that he may lift you up in due time."
1 Peter 5:5-6

Ask yourself, are you ready to humble yourself and risk it all for the Lord, even if it means going through the dirt and grime to get in the presence of your soul mate? To even take it to a deeper level, you must be doing it not only for yourself but your love for another. Remember, Ruth worked for her livelihood and Naomi's. Do you know by doing the little things such as making a simple phone call, leaving a note on someone's door, or cooking a bowl of soup is honorable in the eyes of those watching you? So while you are out there in life working for your dreams, goals, ministry and such, know that you are being watched.

What you do, how you do it and what you speak will get back to the one you may least expect, your Boaz. All of these things work together for your good. Nothing is by chance ... Before you know it guess who will be tapping you on the shoulder? You got it! Your Boaz.

Olivia Stith

Journey of Faith III

BETHLEHEM: SOMETHING FIELDS RIGHT

Chapter 10

He Has You Covered Before He Becomes Your Covering

Things are rolling now! Obviously after talking to the foreman, Boaz went to Ruth himself and let her know that he, as the landowner, wanted her to stay.

"So Boaz said to Ruth, "My daughter, listen to me. Don't go and glean in another field and don't go away from here."
Ruth 2:8

Now Ruth has Boaz's blessings to work in the field. There was no word of mouth from the foreman or the servant girls. It came straight from, as we say, "the horse's mouth." He said what he meant and meant what he said. He wanted her to stay. There was no question about it and it didn't even matter what anyone else thought or said.

Olivia Stith

That's a true sign of a man! And look at the endearing, protective term he uses, "daughter." He doesn't act like a father in a way where he treats her as though she's helpless, but instead in a caring way, while ensuring his daughter safety in the process of her being in the midst of danger. He keeps her close to his own and all negativity at bay so that he can protect and watch over her. Now keep in mind though that neither of them was thinking of marriage at this point.

The key thing on Boaz's mind was protecting this young woman from being taken advantage of by other unsavory men. It was not so much about her becoming his wife but it was his looking out for her well being. We later read that he did this because he knew with Ruth being a widow, she had no male covering and he took her under his wings.

Didn't I tell you before about that humbleness from a woman that lets a man know she is open to him leading her?

When he sees this he goes into a protective and loving mode. In his mind he is thinking, "She's strong and hard working, yet I must protect her from the wolves out there." The men who run game are the ones who may want to take advantage of her but not Boaz. He steps in as a provider and protector. You may be thinking you have a spiritual covering such as a Pastor, a natural father, or a brother, but this type of covering is different. This is one that God is orchestrating for a union of two people to become one, with you being the woman as the weaker vessel to have the covering of the man (when you marry).

"Husbands, in the same way be considerate as you live with your wives, and treat them with respect as the weaker partner and as heirs with you of the gracious gift of life, so that nothing will hinder your prayers."
1 Peter 3:7

Olivia Stith

Now this may surprise you but your Boaz is not going to walk into your life and say, "Boom! You are the one, marry me!" Oh, so many want it that way, but relationships are to be cultivated.

God does things in season for the benefit of the two people. Nothing comes as a guessing game in the kingdom; all things are confirmed. The true motives in a man will be revealed by his heart's actions. If a man is sent to be your covering, he will show responsible and husband-like qualities to you before the big wedding day. He knows how to take control. Now, we are not talking about possessiveness but one of protectiveness. Know the difference; just because he has dominion over a place, doesn't make him domineering, and no man of God will act this way. A man with sincere motives will demonstrate godliness and not sinful, self-centered actions.

You know, we hear a lot of things, but when a man walks in our life and speaks like no other, sister you know we're all ears. It's time to listen! He is one who will come into our life speaking under the anointed power of God and not just speaking flattering words... The concern of his heart is not about his own fleshly desires because it operates out of concern for you as a woman of God.

It's not about him at all and he knows this. God will send that man into your life by His divine authority and have this man operating as more of a spiritual covering than anything. I'm not saying in the natural he will not be assisting you, but the foundation that God is building on first is that which is spiritual. Most of the time we try to focus on the natural and material assets first and then we get with the spiritual. It doesn't work in that manner. As the spiritual is being spoken into a man's heart and mind, the fruit it produces will manifest in the natural.

Olivia Stith

This man will be the one who calls you and suggests you pray and fast together, because it's a form of protection. His interest will be in the work you are doing and he will be like a watchman on the wall of your life. He takes heed to the people who are around you and will voice his opinions on those that he feels may not have your best interest at heart.

It's not that you cannot handle yourself, but he knows as a man that there are certain things he can speak that will carry more authoritative power than a woman standing alone, even though he sees you as a woman of strength. Let's be realistic; there are certain areas in this world that a man makes more secure and comforting for us. We are women, plain and simple. Regardless of how strong we are, God has made man to be our covering and protector in the natural. He has equipped him to be that watchman over His daughters.

A man sent by the Lord will be drawn to take you under his wings. This is God's way of preparing him to have you as a wife. It is also showing you His divine power and authority in that man's life. This man will not have you walking through life aimlessly without direction. Oh no, he will be right there by your side. This man will walk in your life with direction and instructions from God on how to keep you both in a place that you two can work on together.

He wants you working beside him, not necessarily in the same ministry per say, but in all other areas of his life. You will then see how things will start to flow from there. Why is this? God wants to demonstrate that you two can work as a team.

"Do two walk together unless they have agreed to do so?"
Amos 3:3

Notice Boaz didn't stop Ruth from working at all. He just let her know he had her back.

Olivia Stith

You will not stop working in your God given purpose when he comes into your life. The weight of the world will become lighter because the brother is like a protective umbrella over you in the field. Isn't it comforting to know that a man is in your life pushing you on with kingdom power? You know it's God when a brother is extending his hand to help you and not asking for nothing in return. It shows he has respect for you.

You know the amazing thing is this; He is doing this strictly out of his love for the woman who he has come to admire because of her love for God and dedication to her fellow man. He is beginning to see you as a woman like no other. He sees the beauty of you being a humble risk taker and hard worker, yet more importantly he sees the God in you. He truly begins to see you as a blessing!

Chapter 11

It's Time to Follow the Leader and Roll With His Peeps

"Stay here with my servant girls. Watch the field where the men are harvesting, and follow along after the girls.
Ruth 2:8

Well I'm sure Ruth was feeling a bit more secure now that Boaz was looking over her as she worked in the fields. You know, when you out there doing what's expected of you, God will start showing His favor on your life from those around you, including the one He has sent you before. Remember, it's the Lord's plans that are being orchestrated here, even though neither one of you knows the outcome. As we say in the theater, "the stage has been set and the players on are." Be still and watch how things unfold.

Olivia Stith

Now Boaz is not only becoming Ruth's protector, but he has also informed those in his fields not to bother her. Ruth is now officially part of the crew! First Boaz gives her his approval, but notice; he doesn't move her up in position to one of his servant girls. How would Boaz have looked if he had quickly elevated Ruth, who was new to the fields, before someone who had been diligently working in the field for a longer period of time? We know heads would start to turn and roll! To make matters even worse, the environment would have become much more hostile for Ruth to work in. Boaz knew what he was doing. He observes Ruth to see how she functions in this close setting with his workers. So not only is he helping her but he is also keeping peace in his own field. You see, she must prove herself in his vineyard, before advancing. This is symbolic of how life operates for us in the natural and the spiritual as well.

One key thing to remember is that we all have learned from the past. God starts us out working in the smaller things first, whether it's on a job, in ministry or other areas.

We must show faithfulness and humbleness. An appreciative spirit, regardless of our circumstances, is a good steward over what is delegated to it. It brings elevation and elevation in the kingdom comes from above. Once the Lord sees you are faithful in serving him, he can elevate you to the status of a woman ready for one of His sons. He is going to watch how you treat the others around you. Are you one that is able to follow and receive direction without murmuring and complaining? Keep in mind this is something God is looking at. If you can't take directions from God or those leaders who He has placed over you, do you think He is going to release you to man? You have to show Him that you can be responsible and faithful over the blessings He has bestowed upon you as a single woman. Life changes when its no longer just you but two. Matters become more complex and this all takes time to fall into place. In the process of God getting you to this point, it's important to learn and glean in the spirit while He gives you protection. You have to understand that God has it all in control and you can be comforted in knowing His eyes

Olivia Stith

are on you.

Once you have proven yourself, you will be elevated to that "found woman" status and the same things you have been doing all along with Christ in your daily walk will come back full circle with your Boaz. We know it starts off as a friendship, because a man of God has to know who you are as a woman first, before he goes headfirst into a relationship. It would be foolish to jump the gun and say, "This is my wife" and the man doesn't fully know you as a person. He has heard about you, seen you in action, but that one on one time is just beginning.

I'm sure this man is going to spend quality time with you before he starts taking you around and introducing you as a special woman in his life. It has to be a slow pace as you begin to know this person, right? We know we just don't marry a man and live on an island. His life and those in it will have an impact on both your lives. Now I'm not saying they have a say so in your marriage, but honey let's be real, when you start getting to know a man you're going to get to know his family and the rest of the crew.

Now as this happens, you both need to ask, are you able to abide peacefully together around those who are in both of your lives?

I know as women, when we set our eyes on a good man, we want front and center, but a brother has to know you can work with what's in his life. He won't have you in a position to be disrespected or treated unfairly because he has your best interest at heart, even amongst his people. He is not rushing things too fast either but rather taking his time to establish that you have a spot in his life. That shows people around him that he is thinking rationally and using common sense. Everything is not spiritual sister; some things are simply common sense.

Once again that foundation is being built. Can you trust him with the words he speaks? Is his advice one that is advancing you further in your point of life? A man of God is not going to have you just jump out there full fledged without advising you to be watchful. He will not lead you on the wrong path where harm will come to you. There

Olivia Stith

goes that attribute of being the head once again, because his leadership is being portrayed. That which he cares for, he will ensure by all means that it is protected. This is in the natural and the spiritual. He lets people know he is standing by you and trusting you with whatever project you're working on. This brother intercedes in the spirit to make sure you are covered by the power of God from any demonic forces that may want to stop you from progressing. He is moving with the "hands off approach." Not only that, but he connects you with people who are out there doing productive things. These people will yield His fruit in your life because they have proven that they can get the job done. He doesn't have to exert his authority by forcing his friendships upon you because he is humble in his work by advising you to learn from them. Not only is he honoring them and showing respect for whom they are in his life, but it also lets everyone know you are a team player who doesn't have to have the front row seat. You're just appreciative that this man sees something in you that merits favor. You see; it all boils down to this man trusting that the Spirit in him is releasing you to a newer level in his life. Keep in mind, neither one of you are certain of who the other is yet, even though God knows. The one thing that he can vouch for is how you stood out in the crowds and how that moved him to get to know you better. That's a step of elevation because it is taking things to a new level. Once a man starts seeing the favor of God on your life, He will continue releasing this favor! Its time to show him and those around him what you know!

Olivia Stith

CHAPTER 12

Favor is Just Not Fair! You Betta Tell It!

"At this, she bowed down with her face to the ground. She exclaimed, "Why have I found such favor in your eyes that you notice me - a foreigner?" Boaz replied, "I've been told all about what you have done for your mother-in-law since the death of your husband - how you left your father and mother and your homeland and came to live with a people you did not know before.
Ruth 2: 10-11

Ruth was overwhelmed by Boaz's generosity. You hear it all the time, "FAVOR IS NOT FAIR!" Well, what can you say when the favor of God is on your life and its flowing from all over? What makes a man give you favor?

Is it something that you get because we just got it like that? No ma'am! In your dreams! Favor is a fruit of faith that brings forth faithfulness. When you remain faithful to God He gives you favor. Staying trustworthy and humble before Him allows you to receive His favor in spite of your social or economic status. It's not about where you are going or where you came from. No! It's about your attitude in the state you are now. Are you still working as hard? Are you grateful? If you are, watch how the favor of God is manifested in the eyes of others and through their actions. It's strange, but it's true.

It takes strength in the harshest of situations to lift your voice in praise to God. Most waddle in self-pity, which ultimately leads to a spiritual death. Praise God when he allows you to walk through the fire without getting burned. It's amazing to people... This is why when we carry this attribute of Ruth, a foreigner. Remember you are different from the rest.

Olivia Stith

There is something about you that has caught that man's attention in spite of all that has transpired in your life. This is why Boaz was moved with compassion for Ruth. She was a woman who left everything to come to a new life, not knowing what to expect but trusting in God. When a man sees you standing strong in spite of instead of buckling down in defeat, it compels him to you the more. Many times he is moved by compassion to make your load lighter. This is favor.

Think for a minute how you left everything behind and came to this new life in Christ. I'm sure there were friendships you had to sever and even family relations may have become strained because you chose to follow the faith. This is your testimony that Boaz will hear. So girlfriend this new man is not looking at your past, but how he can be effective in your future. He will then look within himself to see how he can make your life and transitions better.

A brother has done his homework; you just may not know it. Then one day while you are sitting here amazed at how a real man is treating you so special, he lets you know. He knows all about you. Honey listen closely, it's just not coming from people around him! News Flash! His source is straight from heaven, through prayer with our heavenly Father, he has gained more knowledge on who you are and what exactly you need. See we are all different. We all come from different backgrounds and experiences. We are in various positions in life and in the body of Christ. Your needs are different from your other sisters so the Lord will send a man. So it's not only work he has to do on the earth but the brother must be in tune with heaven. It's the Lord who is confirming in his spirit that's its okay to trust you with this and move you in this place in his life. A righteous man does not make decisions based on his feelings but on revelations from God.

Also along with taking care of Ruth's natural needs, Boaz began to speak prophetically into her life.

Olivia Stith

"May the LORD repay you for what you have done. May you be richly rewarded by the LORD, the God of Israel, under whose wings you have come to take refuge."
Ruth 2:12

This is powerful right here. Once again we see things moving to a new level. When a brother can speak prophetically into your spirit as no other man has before, your spirit willingly receives. Why? Because he is not speaking things based on his assumptions but from direct utterances of God. Honey, that's more soul soothing than a thousand flattering words. It's great to hear sweet words, but you want to hear words that have power to produce what's being said. Notice as Boaz stated, this is not based on what he can do but the God of Israel. The whole time this man knows it's not him who is truly doing the blessing but God. There goes humbleness even in the man A man must be able to follow God in order to know how to effectively lead you. In hearing from God, he is open to speak prophetically into your life.

The whole time Boaz knew who Ruth was

but he did not reveal it to her. It's a time and place when a man will reveal what is shown to him. Just be patient You see, Boat's focus was not on himself but rather assisting her present needs. Wow, imagine that, a man putting your needs before his own This shows you that his motives are not to gain anything for himself, but instead to push you into the position you are to be. You see, he never knows if God in return will give him "you" You know it's stated, "He who finds a wife finds a good thing and obtains favor with the Lord" Favor given, is favor returned from the Most High.

Now it doesn't end there. Boaz spoke into Ruth's life and Ruth in return speaks into her own life concerning Boaz, right there in front of him Not only that but she is bowed before him in humbleness. Notice the attitude in all this, humbleness and gratitude. Don't you think a brother is in awe of a foreign woman lying at his feet while telling him how blessed she is to have found his favor? His spirit tells him that she is sincere and not about selfish gain. You see, she knows her place and she's content because

Olivia Stith

she knows God has placed her there. Ruth states,

"May I continue to find favor in your eyes, my lord," she said. "You have given me comfort and have spoken kindly to your servant - though I do not have the standing of one of your servant girls."
Ruth 2:12-13

Girlfriend when a man starts speaking life into your spirit, the Lord may use you to bless him as well. It's like a tag team blessing. Amazing how it works... Do you see how it is when a man is truly leading? It's not about telling a woman anything, but showing her. "Look I see this in you and you should too!" This is a man sowing self-esteem into her spirit. This is powerful. He is building her up not only on the outside but the inside too. Now this man has you seeing yourself as one to be favored and you are letting him know you appreciate it. Let him know girlfriend!

Don't let anyone make you feel like you shouldn't boost a man's ego. You continue speaking truthful things about how he's treating you and making you feel. What's wrong with a quick text, a card, an email, or a call on the phone simply saying, "Thanks for being a friend." Sister, when you do it, this is the clincher. Do it without ulterior motives; your ways of operating as a woman is to be led by the Spirit. He will know the difference, trust me. As he pours into you, you pour back into him! You may not be in close to him as some others but you are his Favor-ite girl! All you have to know is - Favor is not fair!

Olivia Stith

Chapter 13

Just A Little Dip and Sip Will Do

Boaz not only offered Ruth the security of being safe while out in the fields, but he ensured during the process of her working that she wouldn't faint from thirst.

"And whenever you are thirsty, go and get a drink from the water jars the men have filled."
Ruth 2:9

After she worked hard all day, he beckoned her to come to the table and eat as much as she liked. So once again we see a man covering her in more than one area - security, stability, comforting, and now he is even feeding her. His allowing her to come and sit amongst others and eat from one of his tables is a pure sign of respect.

"At mealtime Boat said to her, "Come over here. Have some bread and dip it in the wine vinegar." When she sat down with the harvesters, he offered her some roasted grain. She ate all she wanted and had some left over."
Ruth 2:14

Do you see how things are progressing? She may be a foreigner in the land but she is not stranger to him in the spirit, so the favor continues to be manifested in the natural. Did they both not speak this over her life earlier? So now we have Ruth eating at Boaz's table!

Are you ready to eat at your Boaz's table? You know in order to fully keep you nourished a brother must ensure that you have water and bread. Now honey we know in the natural if a man can't afford to feed you, a relationship shouldn't be on your lips. This goes deeper than the everyday eating. It's symbolic of refreshing the spirit and feeding the soul.

Olivia Stith

It's also showing that you are able to sit and eat what he eats and I'm not talking about steak and potatoes. I'm speaking in a sense of life and ministry. Let's first deal with the refreshing that will come from this brother.

We know that the living water is the Spirit of God that refreshes our souls. When we are out there working in the kingdom we must be refreshed by the word of God. Sometimes we have to go and be nourished by others, as Ruth did. Boat offered her refreshment so she wouldn't faint from the heat. A man of God is going to ensure that you get the rest you need when you are busy doing your thing out there. It's not all work, work, and work. It can be draining and you need refreshing to restore your balance. A man who is in tune with your needs will see this. He is going to take it upon himself to make sure an avenue is open so that sometimes you can kick your feet up and just relax.

It may be in a manner of soft meditation, a quiet get away or even him pouring in your spirit. That's the most important thing right there. Is he able to refresh your spirit with the living waters? This is what's going to truly quench your thirst. It's easy to take a sip of water, but when a man knows how to pour back into you when you're tired from the cares of life, that tells it all!

Now that we've talked about water, let's talk about food and eating from the same table. We know food is for nourishment and growth. The man whom God sets you with will be on a certain level in the spirit. He will have a calling on his life that merits him to have a mate that is able to carry the mantel or shall I say, be able to eat what he is eating. For an example, one may be involved with a Pastor. Well, this mantel carries a lot of responsibility and a woman who is, let's says a new babe in Christ on milk, may not be able to take the pressures and responsibilities that come with the position of a pastor's wife. She is not able to eat at his table, or handle the mantel on his life.

Olivia Stith

You must be spiritually yoked as well as equally yoked to avoid serious relationship issues, and it works both ways. If you, as a woman of God, are in a ministry where spiritually you are on meat and you are involved with a man who is still on milk, it will be hard for him to lead you. There would be an unbalance in the spirit. So look and see the type of spiritual meat or bread the brother is eating from. If you feel you are weak in an area, grab that Bible and start chewing on the word. If you hunger and thirst for this state of righteousness, you will be filled.

In the natural Boat offered Ruth food because she was hungry, but in the spirit, a man will want to know if you are able to handle the mantel on his life. He wants to see if you are woman enough to handle what he lays on the table. He's seen you out in the fields doing your thing, but now when it comes time to sit amongst his peers and eat from his table, can you stomach it? Or does your stomach turn and you have to run? Carefully consider these things in this process. If a man is presenting the opportunity to you, he obviously sees the potential in you, to be able to sit beside him and be fed. It gives a man pleasure to be able to sit and nourish his woman. You can take it sister. In fact, you can chew it all and have some left over like Ruth! With all that anointing and blessings, you can't help but share it.

The more time you spend together "eating," the more you two will grow! Isn't that how it works? This is the beginning of a healthy relationship. So when the table is spread before you, prepare to go to that next level, it's your time to sip and dip. Oh yeah, when you get full, you are going to take all that you have acquired and share it with others... Just like Ruth! You can't sit still and not tell it!

Chapter 14

He's a Behind the Scenes Man

"Boat gave orders to his men, "Even if she gathers among the sheaves, don't embarrass her. Rather, pull out some stalks for her from the bundles and leave them for her to pick up, and don't rebuke her."
Ruth 2: 14-16

There is nothing like a man working behind the scenes to ensure things get done for your benefit. Is that a blessing or what? Sounds just like what the Lord has been doing the entire time.

This shows the godliness in Boat because he was acting in the same manner as God did. Do you see the similarities in all of this? The relationship you both possess with Christ will be reflected in your union.

It's not a union of words but actions. I cannot stress this enough... If God is residing and ruling in a person, they will manifest His qualities in their lives.

As God was working things in Boat and Ruth's favor, Boat was doing the same for her. I believe something was sparked inside of this man that he had never experienced before. This new girl bought something new in this brother's life. Once again he is making sure she is cared for and even going the extra mile and instructing his men to intentionally leave stalks for her.

So now, without her even knowing it, the favor is growing! Do you know where it all stemmed from? It stemmed from her obedience and faith.

It manifested from her behind the scenes man, Boat. It takes humility to be a behind the scenes man because one is doing works without being acknowledged. In all actuality, this is how it's supposed to be and a wise man knows this.

Olivia Stith

The Lord looks highly upon those who take it amongst themselves to be a blessing to another and not look to receive high praise because of their deeds. What you do in the dark, God blesses you openly. You see, if a man is always doing things for you to be seen, then he wants to receive self-glory and praise and that's taking the glory from God. God does not share His glory with anyone! For someone to walk around boasting with his or her head held high because they are able to help someone in need is foolish. A godly man knows it's better to receive His kingdom reward, than to seek honor and praise from men. That is exactly what Boat did!

Not only will this brother bless you but he will instruct others to bless you as well.

Have you ever been involved with someone and then all of sudden, doors started to open in your life that weren't open or even there before?

Opportunities began to stand before you and all you had to do was reach out and take advantage of them. When all this happens you will see growth in your life again. I'm sure you will get to a place like Ruth did where you fall on your knees and praise God because once things start happening like this to us, it becomes almost unbelievable. Truly, you will wonder and ask, "why all the favor?" Well, because it's your season and unbeknownst to you, the Lord is using a special man to bring his promise to you to past.

You're surprised that a man will come and take you under his wings and make it his mission to see that the desires of your heart are met. In this day and time someone doing such great works truly has to be God sent! These days most people want tit for tat and will let you know too, so for someone to just step up and be motivated to basically give away their prized possessions to further your cause is priceless.

Olivia Stith

Sister, you best know this man is even telling people around him to keep quiet, because he understands that the glory and praise goes to God. It's not a time for him to act big headed. Even those around him may try to boost him up and discourage him from being a blessing, but like Boat, this man has a "take charge" attitude. This is his life, his field and he is the one directing how things flow. This is a man that has kingdom authority and when he speaks it's not just plain words being spoken, but the Holy Ghost backs and powers them. Watch the manifestations. What goes on behind the scenes eventually will be seen in the forefront. You didn't know...?

Chapter 15

Hmmm... Girlfriend I See a Change!

There are no ifs or ands about it; when happenings such as what was going on with Ruth start showing in one's life, people are definitely going to take notice. As changes and shifts take place in your life, it's going to affect others around you. When Ruth obtained favor from God and Boat, so did Naomi.

"She carried it back to town, and her mother-in-law saw how much she had gathered. Ruth also brought out and gave her what she had left over after she had eaten enough. Her mother-in-law asked her, "Where did you glean today? Where did you work? Blessed be the man who took notice of you"
Ruth 2:18-19

Olivia Stith

Naomi knew somewhere that Ruth had obtained favor from the increase of goods and food she was bringing into the house. Do you see a pattern here? Sacrificing for others, favor, blessings, sacrificing for others, favor, blessings... Okay now in that equation we don't see anything about relationship, or getting a man right? Its not about anyone thinking on a husband, wife or such, it's simply about being blessed because you are out in the field working for the kingdom and God is getting the full glory in all of this first. Even from those people around you... You are out there sacrificing your own comfort to be a blessing, while you lighten the burden of someone else. In the process you are being blessed because of your blessing someone else. It's a trickle-down effect and everyone around you will begin to see it.

You can't put food in the body and not see it grow. Remember, this new man is bringing food to your soul, he is taking away a thirst that no other man could and you are not only growing but also glowing. The pressure of changing who you are for a man is not there, because God has not put the focus on you and him, but on Him above. You both realize that this meeting of your souls is an honor that God has orchestrated. Since it is of Him, a change will come. It's so noticeable that those around you cannot help but speak on it, just as Naomi did. Naomi begins speaking blessings over Boat without even knowing he is the landowner. There it goes! You don't have to have your name on a blessing as long as God knows you the giver.

"The LORD bless him!" Naomi said to her daughter-in-law. "He has not stopped showing his kindness to the living and the dead." She added, "That man is our close relative; he is one of our kinsman-redeemers."
Ruth 2:20

Naomi had been with Ruth since the deaths of their husbands and I know they endured hardships together.

Olivia Stith

Naomi knew the risk Ruth faced out there and what normally would be expected of a foreign woman. She knew working the small job would usually get the scraps, but here comes Ruth with the overflow. This was not the norm. This is why Naomi exclaimed in awe that this man would be blessed. The actions of the man God is sending in your life is going to outshine any other man you have ever been with. This is one of the signs that you will know. I'm sure there are many men who have done you a favor, but how many have obtained divine favor from God and have shown it to you? You see, there's a difference when a man works for you on behalf of God's favor. Many men do things for you out of selfish motives, while others will do things because they might simply feel sorry for you. However, when the favor of God is on your life and that special man sees it, he is going to be compelled to shower you with more because of his love for God and also the God he sees in you. It's not a one-time thing; this is favor with a consistency. When you are constantly getting something put on you, don't you have an overflow? One beautiful thing about this is people will see it!

That's right; those in your own home, church, ministry and job will see it. It cannot be denied. Your mindset has begun to change. That sadness that once was in the heart from the past pains (remember Ruth husband had recently died) is diminishing and you are speaking positive things over your life. Now you are being compelled to make the best of things regardless of your circumstances. Your life is getting better and you are able to spread it amongst those around you. Joy spreads... Look at Naomi. I'm sure after feeling God had left her, joy and hope was restored in her life. It's a relief to know that when you feel God has left you, He appears and shows you through others, He is still there.

You see, all of this was more than a relationship being built. God was continually building on His relationship with them all, Ruth, Naomi and Boat. God never left them.

Olivia Stith

This is why in the midst of God having you cross paths with that special man, the changes in your life are for the good, and are positively affecting those around you. Spread the good news, not about you per say, but how God has just blessed you with a friend and the impact has been life changing. The opportunities and doors that are opening for you must be kept open for others. The man is the tool that God is using to not only bless you but your fellow brothers and sisters as well. This builds unity, not only in you two as a couple, but also to those around you. Now not only have his friends noticed the change in him, but they have begun to give you honor and respect too. This feeds into those in your life because they now begin to honor him. Do you see how God is bringing the two together? Once again, in due season the plan of God will begin to be revealed and there is nothing people can say, because the proof is in the pudding!

Chapter 16

Geesh, Now You Tell Me

When we see people changing around us, usually curiosity gets the best of us, especially when it brings favor not only upon their life, but ours as well. Naomi was overwhelmed with the magnitude of Ruth's blessings and favor. She simply did what most of us would do,

"Her mother-in-law asked her, "Where did you glean today? Where did you work? Blessed be the man who took notice of you" Then Ruth told her mother-in-law about the one at whose place she had been working. "The name of the man I worked with today is Boaz," she said.

Ruth 2:19

Olivia Stith

Wow, there it is! Things are ready to shift again – this time with the drop of a name. I could imagine the look on Naomi's face when Ruth said this. The wheels are really turning now! God's plan is ready to progress to the next level, because now Naomi sees the opportunity that God is laying before them and how the plan of God is starting to unfold.

Boaz was one of the kinsman-redeemers in the family. Let it be known that a kinsman-redeemer had special standing in the Jewish family. This was a male relative in the family whose responsibility was to save the family name. They would buy land that may have been lost by relatives as well as family members who were sold into slavery. These men could choose to marry the widows of the deceased so that the family name could be preserved.

Basically they were the ones who had the ability to keep the lineage and family inheritance flowing when another could not. You know that night rejoicing must have been going on between the two women. Things were set right? Well…not so fast. Things still had to be in place, but the great thing about it was Ruth now knew who Boaz was through Naomi. When you testify of God's goodness, you never know what token of blessing lies within your words.

Another thing, Do you see how important it is to cling to your Naomi? The Naomi in your life is a guide and an accountability partner. More importantly she is able to guide you in areas she has already treaded, such as marriage. She teaches you how operate in elegance and grace. You begin developing yourself into a woman of purpose who possesses patience. Sometimes moving too fast will get you into a hot mess and lagging behind will cause you to miss out. It's vital to keep those listening ears open. Once the revelation of Boaz was put forth, things started to take a new direction.

Olivia Stith

Put yourself in Ruth's place for a moment. Those whom God has appointed to be your spiritual mentors or guides will start to see the transformations in your life after this special Boaz has entered your life. You are more carefree and fully spirited. Some may think it's a phase you're going through, but they know when it's genuine. They know the tactics of the enemy and the ways of the Lord. It's called discernment, sistah. Not much gets past them. They may tell you, "this is a worthy man who is showing himself to be one of noble character, judging by the way he is treating you." Or, "Hey, this may be your husband Ms. Lady!" Your Naomi will see that this brother has been uplifting you and it seems that he has surpassed the foolish games played by the men in your past.

Now your heart is jumping because you know you have met your "potential" husband, but what do you do? Do you run and tell him? Should you call your sister girls' on the phone? I mean, what better moment is it when God starts revealing that your heart may have found its mate?

You want to tell the world right? I'm sure Ruth was bubbling over, knowing for herself that she had a position in Boaz's life that she was not even aware of. I would have been overjoyed and gushing too! Hey, you've just been given a great word of encouragement from your mentor or leader - but sit still for a moment. This is not the time to mess up now sista! You don't know yet if that man is ready for you. What about the other sisters who work beside you and may have their eyes on him? Can you imagine Ruth running out to the servant girls gloating about her status of being able to be redeemed by Boat? Or even worse, if she had went to Boat and demanded his attention. It would have been a mess because God had not instructed her to do such a thing. Sometimes God will give you information to sit on. Things may look in order to you, but they may not be. Hmmm, these are things you will need to ponder. This is why God has put that Naomi in your life so you wouldn't go out there and make a silly schoolgirl move. Instead of telling the world, she starts telling Naomi more about Boat.

Olivia Stith

Then Ruth, the Moabitess said, "He even said to me, "Stay with my workers until they finish harvesting all my grain."
Ruth 2:21

She kept what she knew between her and her mentor. It still may not be the time for you to make that move. Learn from that and know that God, in His time, will reveal to you your position in a man's life. It seems like it will take forever to get to him right? Be patient God will not have you sitting around guessing and waiting forever. He has just proven that. Remember, you are dealing with a man who has character and does things in order. While you sit and meditate on this news that God has revealed to you, do as Naomi instructed Ruth. Go and get back to doing your normal duties... Continue working in the field!

I know to most of us, that's not what we want to hear. Shoot, you just found out a man can rightfully take you as his wife and away from those hot fields and you can't jump on it? That's right; you're not jumping on it – you're going to listen to your Naomi!

Why not take the direction of someone who has been steering you on the right path all along? You have trusted the God in her this long, so why stop now? So although you might be anxious and giddy, right now your normal life must go on... you gotta go right back out there with the crowds and guess what? Mums the word!

When God reveals to us things such as a man being our potential mate, it's enough to send us into a state of euphoria, but don't lose your mind. We have to keep things in perspective and meditate on them as Mary did when the angel revealed she would have baby Jesus. Sister you can't run and tell it all or you may mess yourself up. So hold tight and stay in the place. Don't lose your place in the field! Keep going on working and doing your thing. You know that life is changing and in time you will be able to shout it off the rooftops.

Olivia Stith

Just trust that God is working this for your good! Keep in mind this revelation of how Boat came when Ruth returned from the field into Bethlehem. When you take time from everything and sit before God in His presence, He will reveal to you who that man of God is. So now you know to get back to work. The best is yet to come!

Chapter 17

My Lips are Sealed

"Naomi said to Ruth her daughter-in-law, "It will be good for you, my daughter, to go with his girls, because in someone else's field you might be harmed." "So Ruth stayed close to the servant girls of Boaz to glean until the barley and wheat harvests were finished. And she lived with her mother-in-law."
Ruth 2:22-23

One of the most powerful things you will need to know as a woman is when to open your mouth and when to keep it closed. This goes along with knowing when to act on a situation at the right time, when you know you are right about a situation or when you know you have an upper hand and others may not know it. Talking and moving too fast will send you reeling out of place with those around you and God.

Olivia Stith

Hasty actions and a fast tongue have caused many of us at times, to lose plenty of blessings, including what could have been a great mate. Don't worry, God is merciful and is known for giving second chances. So a word to the wise is, when the Spirit reveals to you something as powerful as who the man of God is in your life, but tells you to keep silent, girl you better hush! Keep moving forward while waiting on God at the same time and trust there's a reason behind it all.

It would have been out of Ruth's character, after Boaz had seen of her and the workers, to come bouncing on the field and screaming she has a right to be redeemed by Boaz.

This lets you know the two women trusted that God, in His time, would let them know when to act. You see Ruth was in a tight situation.

Boaz had already instructed the men to leave her alone and told her to follow the servant girls. Obviously they saw she had favor in his eyes and who knows what else was going on in the back of their minds?

You know how some people get when someone in authority gives someone else privileges and in their eyes the person doesn't necessarily deserve it. Well, we know it's not up to us to decide who deserves privileges; it's up to God. If you are the one who the favor is being bestowed upon then you know you must carry yourself in a peaceful manner or drama will ensue. This is why your mouth needs to be closed most of the time.

Olivia Stith

I know that there are many women out there waiting for the right man to find them. We work side by side with many of them at our jobs and in our church families too. They are our sisters, cousins, bosses, friends, etc. There are plenty of women around us who are daughters of the "Most High" waiting on their season. These same women are the ones, along with us, who mingle with the brothers.

This is just like the actions of the servant girls, with Ruth, when Boaz came around.

Some of these women have been in the lives of these men longer than we have, but God has not put them together. Honey, we know when a new sister comes on the scene, eyes look and attitudes can fly.

We may not want to admit it but some of us see it as an added piece of competition, instead of a fellow sister in Christ. Let's keep it real! That type of thinking is straight from Moab. And aren't we past that phase? Of course we are! The reason most women think that way is because there is a man shortage, but let me give this piece of info to you. There is no shortage in the kingdom of God! That's the foolish way of thinking and will cause you to stay single. If God has a man for you, then He has a man for you, even if He has to breathe in the dust and make one. God's standards are not based on worldly statistics at all, so keep that in mind.

Drama will start flying all over the place. Why? Simply because every one's mind is not as stable as yours may be. There may be people working beside you but that doesn't necessarily mean they are working with you, does it? The Lord knows this and in order to keep your character and name clean, stay put. Remember, that man is out there watching what you do with the people you associate with, especially those in his camp.

Olivia Stith

This is why you can't run and tell everyone your business. The next thing you know folks will be scheming and praying maledictions and all kinds of things against you.

I know it must have been challenging for Ruth to step on the field and take the backseat by following women around, especially when she, in her rightful position, could be the wife of the owner of the field.

Whew, how many of us could have done that? I can imagine that women knew Boaz was single and because of the kindhearted manner he treated his workers, naturally he would draw admiration from them. I'm sure many a days while sipping on water, the women probably were giggling and talking about Boaz in Ruth's presence. I mean that's normally how we behave behind closed doors, let's keep it real.

A single, successful businessman, who treats people well, that's definitely a topic of conversation, but Ruth had to follow instruction. Naomi told her to hang with the girls and keep working in the fields. Ruth was obedient and this is exactly what she did without mentioning a thing to Boaz or the girls. Girlfriend, you don't have to announce your business on the bullhorn when the Lord has confirmed things to you. There is no need to prove a thing to anyone but God! You will need this type of self-control, especially if you have a man who is in ministry or a job that requires him being in the presence of other women, because nothing is worse than an insecure woman. There's no need for insecurity when God has displayed numerous times to you and those around you, the spot that you hold in this brother's life. Keep the peace and allow God to continue His work to bring it all full circle. In your secret place get your praise on because soon the trumpets will start to blow and you will be on center stage because God will place you there! Let Him tell you when to move and don't breathe a word!

Olivia Stith

Journey of Faith IV

BETHLEHEM: FIELD-IN FOR ONE ANOTHER

Chapter 18

Let Wisdom Dress You

One day Naomi her mother-in-law said to her, "My daughter, should I not try to find a home for you, where you will be well provided for?"
Ruth 3:1

Finally the time has come for Ruth to rest. Rest meaning, it was now time for her to settle down with a husband and move on with her life. I'm not sure how much time had passed, but obviously it was now time in Naomi's mind for Ruth to leave her home to get one of her own. Ruth had shown her loyalty and commitment and it was time to move forward. Naomi knew now was the time to go to Boaz and request that he marry Ruth based on their Jewish customs, being he was a redeemer of their family.

Olivia Stith

"Tonight he will be winnowing barley on the threshing floor. Wash and perfume yourself, and put on your best clothes. Then go down to the threshing floor, but don't let him know you are there until he has finished eating and drinking. When he lies down, note the place where he is lying. Then go and uncover his feet and lie down. He will tell you what to do."
Ruth 3:3-4

Things may appear to be taboo in our day and age, an older woman telling a younger woman to dress up real pretty, wait until a man finishes his drink, and then lay at his feet. I know some of the old church mothers would be cringing at this thought in those times, but it was not as we see it today. Naomi was a virtuous woman and Ruth was one of integrity as well, neither would have done anything to tarnish their name.

"I will do whatever you say," Ruth answered."
Ruth 3:5

Ruth trusted Naomi's advice and Naomi trusted that Ruth would do the right thing. It was time for her to move to the next level in her relationship with Boaz and what better person to advise her than Naomi. The time will come my sister when you will have to let it be known to the man, that you are available and interested in him. Now I know this can seem tricky but it's not. This is he time where you must be speaking to and getting direction from God Himself. God will let you know how, where and when to express taking the relationship to a new level. Now some may say it's up to the man to bring marriage to the woman's attention, but let's be real. A man cannot ask us anything, if we do not let him know we're interested. Boaz did not know that Ruth was interested in him at this time. We will find out later why he didn't approach her first. Ladies there is nothing wrong with letting a brother know you're interested in him, if God has shown you that it's now the season for you to be released to be a wife. In this season of being in the field, you have been working alone and doing things for yourself for a long time. Well, in the proper time God will let you know it's your season to speak openly to your Boaz about your feelings. Be subtle, feminine and bold. Ruth boldly laid at Boaz's feet. Now we know you will not go to the extremes of laying at his feet in the natural, but your feelings are what I'm speaking on. A man is not a mind reader like most of us desire, even though he may be thinking the same thing as us. He may not approach you for various reasons and the only way to get to the brunt of the matter is to approach him. That seems a little forward to some, but with God on your side and the wise advice of those around you, what do you have to lose? Remember, there's also a way to do it.

Naomi gives Ruth specific directions on how, when and where to approach Boaz. Once again here goes a wise woman giving directions but, you have to be ready and prepared for this! It may sound strange to most but this is how the customs went when a widow put in her bid to be redeemed. Naomi gave Ruth specific instructions and this time she advises Ruth to dress up for the occasion!

Part of getting the man to a certain point is dealing with the natural as well. I know most you know that. What this means is show your feminine side - , beautify yourself, loosen up, relax and just be you. We know many times when we are working or doing many other activities, we get lost into the daily mechanics. We walk around in sweats and uniforms or work clothes, running here and there taking care of business, but rarely show that soft, relaxed lady side. I mean life is fast pace I know, but when it comes to a man, remember that brothers are visual creatures. It's time to show him that Sister Sue is a vivacious, beautiful woman. Get your nails done, swoop that hair up, find you a sassy dress and let him know, "Brother we need to talk." Make arrangements to go to a nice restaurant and you set the tone for that all important conversation. Come on sister, you are already bold, daring and a risk taker! You are a daughter of the King who has been given his permission to be a wife to one of his sons. It's ok to press forward! Girl what are you waiting for?

Olivia Stith

Now before you jump in that car, remember that you must still operate in holiness. You are a woman of noble character, so it's not a matter of getting in a heated situation that will lead to lustful sex. We are speaking of displaying your femininity without it producing lust. We are not trying to get the man's eyes to pop out his head, but to get him to see that soft, feminine side of you. He already knows how beautiful you are on the inside and out, but this mode I'm speaking of is a relaxing one. No holds barred! The titles and the collars come off (no pun intended) so you can see the natural person without anything else between. This is what you want the brother to see. A man wants a woman who is saved, sassy and sensuous and who allows wisdom to guide her. You will know how to step into that room and get his attention because honey you are ready to have the talk of a lifetime with him.

So prepare yourself and choose a time that is comfortable for both of you. One where you are both alone, in a place where the focus is just you and him. The candles are flickering, the food is good and you look and smell like a million bucks. Honey, the best thing is that God has given you His stamp of approval. Now you know when our Father gives us the okay on a man, it's on sister. Its time to give the brother a good talking to!

Chapter 19

Feet Don't Fail Me Now!

"So she went down to the threshing floor and did everything her mother-in-law told her to do. Ruth approached quietly uncovered his feet and lay down."
Ruth 3:6-7

It's not surprising that Ruth did exactly what Naomi told her to do. She was not going to miss out on her blessing. Following divine direction is so important in this phase of your life. So many women mess up at this point. They rush right in and do things their own way instead of following the instructions that God has given them. Trust that God who knows the mind of the man has sent you. The Lord knows what it takes to gain his attention and He will use others to guide you. He will continue to guide you as well. After you lay things at the man's feet, continue to lie at the feet of Jesus.

This will keep things in focus and also help you keep your mind from taking things into an area it shouldn't wander into. God is moving on your behalf as long as you allow Him to.

"When Boaz had finished eating and drinking and was in good spirits, he went over to lie down at the far end of the grain pile."
Ruth 3:7

Look how God is working this. Boaz has finished eating and drinking and is in a relaxed mood and he reclines by the grains on the threshing floor. God has put him in good spirits but he's not drunk my friend. He had to be alert to protect his grain pile. The reason they laid by the grains after the threshing was to protect it from being stolen. So there is a man once again protecting what's his and making sure nothing happens to it. Faithfully he laid right there beside it. Now if he is doing that for grain, imagine what he would do for his wife.

Olivia Stith

Let God set the mood before you make a move is what we see here. He is the one to relax the mood, because He is the one who is working this from the beginning. When God gives you the okay to proceed further into your relationship with this man, He will have the groundwork laid way before you even get there. All the tension, confusion and such will not be there, because the Spirit of God is going to give him a sense of peace. Remember, God has already set you before him in the fields and this man is already comfortable with you, taking care of you, ensuring others give you respect, and helping you through your trials and tribulations which all contributes to the foundation already being laid out. The qualities that he needs to be a husband are already being demonstrated over and over by now. Now you both have to acknowledge that this is what God wants. You are out of the field now! You are taking a rest to focus on what will be a new phase in your life. So prepare yourself as Ruth did.

"Ruth approached quietly, uncovered his feet and lay down."
Ruth 3:7

Carefully observe how Ruth moved... Quietly. She didn't rush or jump into anything. She quietly approached where he was. This is how you must be in dealing with this Man of God. You have to know how to approach him in a quiet manner and not just jump and throw something on him suddenly. Timing, timing. You already know what you are going to say, but you must know when it's the right time to say it. You are already in place. It's now just a matter of knowing when to speak. When a man feels you are rushing and pushing something on him, he will run. It's not you who will inform him of who you are, but it's God that will let him know who you are. You are simply there to let him know that you are available. Sounds confusing? Keep reading and you will see.

"In the middle of the night something startled the man, and he turned and discovered a woman lying at his feet."
Ruth 3:8

Olivia Stith

There it is! Something woke the man up but, it wasn't Ruth! I truly believe it was God who woke Boaz. God woke Boaz to see that a woman was laying at his feet. Do you see now? God will awaken that man to say, "Look there is a woman laying at your feet." My, my, my... Look at God. In the natural, he was resting after a night of eating and drinking, then later watching over his merchandise. Now, let's take it to the spiritual. This man has been eating from the Master's table while feasting on the Word of God and being refreshed by the Spirit. Wait a minute... This is the very same woman who had helped him obtain what he was watching over. Remember Ruth worked in that field beside him. You will have worked side by side with that man in helping him obtain things too, because God has put you together as a team, in order to show that the two of you are able to walk together. So now, here he is being a watchman over what God has blessed him with, but the blessing is more than just material things or ministry. He has a wife laying at his feet and God is ready to let him know just that. God is awakening that man to who you are! But you know what? That can be startling to a man too! Imagine God letting a brother know, it's time to make that move. That's a big step, so he may be a little nervous because this a new thing, but trust in God that He will give this man comfort, insight and support in knowing what to do. Remember Naomi's words, "He will know what to do." Trust me, a man will know what to do when God says, "There she is." You just wait and see.

Olivia Stith

Chapter 20

Laying Down with Nothing, Getting Up with Everything!

"Who are you?" he asked." I am your servant Ruth," she said. "Spread the corner of your garment over me, since you are a kinsman-redeemer."
Ruth 3:9

When Boaz woke up, he was startled to see a woman at his feet. One reason he was surprised was that field workers normally did not come to this spot, just the owners who were watching their grain. Ruth, as we know, was no ordinary woman. She treaded in places and did things most women were afraid to do. What drove her was her trust in God. This was proved in her loyalty to those whom she trusted and her strong belief that God was her provider. Now, aren't you just like that? You definitely should be!

Ruth let it be known who she was, his servant. Not only that but she knew this was the time to let it be known that she was ready to be redeemed. She laid at his feet and laid it all on the table. Now when the redeemer threw his cloak over the woman requesting to be redeemed, that was his sign that he wanted to marry her. Alrighty now!

Now when you go lay before this man (not literally) let him know who you are. Remember to allow your spirit to be humble while your body carries that femininity. This is the time when you combine your humbleness and femininity together for the man to see what he is getting girlfriend!

Take note that not only was Boaz surprised, but he also didn't recognize Ruth; he had never seen her so dressed up and beautiful. He saw her in a new light. It's time now for the man to see you in a new light. My sister this is your time to shine! He sees you in a new light and you are pleasing to his eyes.

Olivia Stith

Remember, God has awakened him to who you are. Not only are you glowing on the outside, but your inner beauty is showing as well. He may even look at you strangely. Imagine the look of a man who recognizes for the first time, "This is the woman I want to marry." Oh, how beautiful you will be in that man's eyes.

Now that God has opened this man to you, it's time to pour into him and let him know how you feel. Ruth let Boaz know she wanted to be redeemed and I'm sure Boaz not only was amazed at her beauty but also pleasantly surprised at the words that came out of her mouth.

"The LORD bless you, my daughter," he replied. "This kindness is greater than that which you showed earlier: You have not run after the younger men, whether rich or poor."
Ruth 3:10

Boaz was simply in awe that Ruth wanted him to redeem her.

In fact, there goes the term "daughter" again, representing what we know as newness and young in spirit. Didn't I tell you men see this? Look at how Boaz recognizes that he is the one that is favored. He lets her know that what she said surpassed all she had done before. Imagine a woman of integrity, character and godliness standing before a man and saying, "I honor you as the one I desire to be my husband." This brother has found favor. Your Boaz will recognize that God had blessed him with someone beyond his dreams, and may even feel undeserving. He will be humbled at the thought that God sees him as worthy of having you. Boaz thought a woman like Ruth would desire a younger man, but he was wrong. Remember that you want an older man in spirit and not a young, unseasoned one. You want an experienced Boaz!

Boaz speaks like some men today who actually think many women in churches today want men who have the big cars, are young flamboyant speakers, and the next America Top Model instead of a

Olivia Stith

man seasoned in the word, and stable in his life and in his walk with Christ. And sometimes they are right! Many sisters, sad to say, are running after worldly, young unstable men and finding out in the end that it's not worth the trouble. Remember, you are a foreigner girlfriend. You're different. You don't desire that type of man; you want a stable and strong man in Christ. So you choose Boaz over the rest of the crowd, and he is truly honored in knowing you have chosen him. The whole time Boaz had eyes on Ruth, he was thinking that she wouldn't want him. But wow! It's amazing how God works.

Well, all it took was Ruth letting him know that this is what she wanted and Boaz letting her know he was willing to redeem her. He was willing to do this because not only did he know she was a woman of noble character, but people in the city knew as well.

"And now, my daughter, don't be afraid. I will do for you all you ask. All my fellow townsmen know that you are a woman of noble character."
Ruth 3:11

Your Boaz will have no qualms about making you his helpmate and everyone will know he has found himself a queen. The foundation has already been set, but there still is more that must be dealt with. That's right sister, it's not over yet. There are still more matters to handle even after you both have agreed to be husband and wife! Boaz wanted Ruth to be his wife, but he let her know it was another man who could claim her first. He would have to go before this man first to get his approval to release Ruth.

Olivia Stith

"Although it is true that I am near of kin, there is a kinsman-redeemer nearer than I. Stay here for the night, and in the morning if he wants to redeem, good; let him redeem. But if he is not willing, as surely as the LORD lives I will do it. Lie here until morning." So she lay at his feet until morning, but got up before anyone could be recognized; and he said, "Don't let it be known that a woman came to the threshing floor." He also said, "Bring me the shawl you are wearing and hold it out." When she did so, he poured into it six measures of barley and put it on her."
Ruth 3: 12-15

Two things to notice here - he didn't try to put pressure on her to be intimate; he only let her know he wanted her to be his wife. Behind closed doors your Boaz will still treat you as a holy vessel even though you two have both agreed to be together. He will keep you honorable because he is a man of honor.

Secondly, he assured that she got out of the place where they had slept before anyone saw her, which would have tarnished her name. Again he was mindful of her honor. Is that a man looking out for a woman or what? And even before she goes, he gives her more provisions to take with her. Likewise, your Boaz will not leave you empty but continue to fill you and make you complete, because it's God that is working in him. Look at how Ruth laid down with nothing, but the sister got up with everything! It was just going to take more patience and time.

Now even though the agreement had been made, Boaz understood that there was a time for everything, and all things had to be done in order. He still had to go before God's counsel to make his intentions known. Your Boaz will also do things in order. What you need to do is trust the man of God as he takes matters into his hands, by keeping the faith that it will all work for the good of you both.

Chapter 21

Is Patience Part of Your Virtue?

"When Ruth came to her mother-in-law, Naomi asked,"How did it go, my daughter?" Then she told her everything Boaz had done for her and added, "He gave me these six measures of barley, saying, 'Don't go back to your mother-in-law empty-handed.' *"* *Then Naomi said, "Wait, my daughter, until you find out what happens. For the man will not rest until the matter is settled today."*

Ruth 3:16-18

I can imagine how Ruth felt walking back home to Naomi. I'm sure Ruth was feeling a bit discouraged, as soon as you think things are settled here comes the whammy.

We know the whammy was the fact that another man had a right to have her hand in marriage. After all the preparation, beautifying herself and laying at the man's feet, she still had to wait to see even if the marriage was going to happen. Wow, that's rough on a sister! So she begins to explain it all to Naomi. God bless Naomi once again for being the voice of reason as she tells Ruth to be patient. Look at the power in her wisdom and encouragement. Naomi kept Ruth's hope alive. Ruth's loyalty and support revived Naomi out of her pain, so now it was Naomi's turn to revive Ruth's spirit and let her know there was still hope. Ruth just had to be patient and wait.

When you are out there waiting for things to happen after you and your Boaz have agreed to be together, keep the faith when things have to be set in order. Get around your Naomi and continue to be encouraged, even when things seem to be flowing in a positive manner and then a bump in the road comes.

Olivia Stith

It can be discouraging when you have gone out and worked so hard for things to come together in your life and once you meet the man of your dreams, setbacks begin to happen. It can be a variety of things, from material things, to spiritual issues that need to be put in place before the actual union takes place. Despite the hindrance you must keep the faith! This is the time, more than ever, that you should have faith and trust in the man whom you will call your husband. You want him to lead a life of order and guess what? He knows the order of how things must go.

Boaz knew that another man had a right to Ruth's hand and he had to make sure, legally, that things were done in order. Legally in the natural and spiritual, things have to be done in order. First you want that man to have accountability of his actions and words to you, God and man.

This man should be leaning on the foundation of his leadership, his parents if he has any, and letting them know that he intends on marrying you - not only his parents but your parents too.

I believe this is the way that God has always intended it to be. We must allow the man to step in and be held in a manner of accountability. Now we are not speaking on getting approvals because we know some people will never approve of anything, but I'm speaking of those who are spiritual mentors and others who have your best interest at heart, people whose thoughts and decisions are based on God's word and not their own opinions. People who will ensure the courtship and marriage will be entered into with all areas covered by both. This is the time when you both may go to marital counseling or things of this nature.

The most important thing of all is that the man has to stand before God, who will hold him to the greatest accountability. This is the time when he should be laying before God in preparation for the position of priest over his household.

We know God has confirmed you as his wife, but it's time for him to go to God and acknowledge that he wants to have one of His daughters.

Olivia Stith

The one who has the full authority over your life, Jesus Christ, has to be the one to bless this union most of all. He is the one that man has to stand before and let him know how he intends to honor and cherish you as a woman of God, to move you in a place of Christ that will elevate you to places you have never been before.

This is why we must be patient and wait on the Lord to finalize things. It is an honor when a man wants to make sure everything is okay and get the approval of those whom he holds dear. This is not a behind the scenes deal at all. This is a holy union that is ready to take place before God and man. Trust God and have faith while your future mate prepares the gates for you to walk through.

Chapter 22

No Man Can Stand In His Shoes

"Boaz took ten of the elders of the town and said, "Sit here," and they did so. Then he said to the kinsman-redeemer, "Naomi, who has come back from Moab, is selling the piece of land that belonged to our brother Elimelech. I thought I should bring the matter to your attention and suggest that you buy it in the presence of these seated here and in the presence of the elders of my people. If you will redeem it, do so. But if you will not, tell me, so I will know. For no one has the right to do it except you, and I am next in line." "I will redeem it," he said."
Ruth 4:2-4

Boaz was a man of his word, especially the word he had promised Ruth. He got the elders and the kinsman-redeemer together in front of witnesses.

Olivia Stith

Things were at a crunch with him, because as we know he was not the one who had the first choice of marrying Ruth. Another man had the right to marry Ruth first. Naturally, to acquire land and enlarge his estate was pleasing to this man and he decided he wanted to redeem Naomi's family. Wow, another blow to the relationship of Ruth and Boaz it would seem, but God was leading Boaz in what to say and when to say it. Boaz then speaks out...

"Then Boaz said, "On the day you buy the land from Naomi and from Ruth the Moabitess, you acquire the dead man's widow, in order to maintain the name of the dead with his property."
Ruth 4:5

Boaz knew the man would not want to share his wealth with Ruth and whatever children came from the union, for this was apart of the law. Boaz knew the man did not want to give up his life and riches. You see how it turns out when you allow a man to work the Master's plan?

At this, the kinsman-redeemer said, "Then I cannot redeem it because I might endanger my own estate. You redeem it yourself. I cannot do it." So the kinsman-redeemer said to Boaz, "Buy it yourself." And he removed his sandal.
Ruth 4:6,8

This was God's divine plan and when God is working on something in your life as spiritually rich as a relationship, no one can change it. This man could not walk in Boaz's shoes! He had no choice but to give Boaz the land and Ruth's hand in marriage. It was a done deal. Ruth was redeemed!

The same thing is happening with you today. Your Boaz is standing before witnesses letting them know how he wants to redeem you and have you as his wife. Let me explain redeeming. It's not about land and money now.

Olivia Stith

This man is telling the world that he is ready to take your hand and walk with you in a holy union. All of your pains from the past, such as bad relationships are all behind you, because they are being cleaned with a new slate. This new slate is a new man in your life. You no longer are being held captive by these things because a new man, who has the authority to speak healing into your pains through praying you through the storms, is now in your life. This man can hold your hands through the dark times and guide you to His light. He has let it be known to God and to man that he is ready for the responsibility. He acquired your body, soul and spirit willingly. No other man can step up to the plate and do this. He has the God given right!

This man was hand picked from God to be your natural redeemer. This all stems from your relationship with the Redeemer, Jesus Christ.

He paid the price and set you free long, long ago. Now He has released you to be with someone who He knows will treat you as a true woman of God.

This person will walk with you in the kingdom and love you just as He first loved you. Praise God for this! From the beginning it was ordained and now God has allowed it manifest. You should be getting your praise on. Shout it out of the gates, you have been redeemed! Go get your shout on girlfriend. I'm shouting with ya!

Chapter 23

A Promise Fulfilled

"So Boaz took Ruth and she became his wife. Then he went to her, and the LORD enabled her to conceive, and she gave birth to a son. The women said to Naomi:" Praise be to the LORD, who this day has not left you without a kinsman-redeemer. May he become famous throughout Israel! He will renew your life and sustain you in your old age. For your daughter-in-law, who loves you and who is better to you than seven sons, has given him birth."
Ruth 4:13-15

God is faithful to those who trust in Him. The woman who was the foreigner, working the least position amongst women, was now holding the heart of the landowner.

Naomi, Ruth and Boaz all received their promises from the Lord whom they trusted. Ruth found her Boaz and Boaz found his wife. Naomi found that her legacy did continue through a daughter in law. God is faithful to you as well as those who have their Boaz and for those of us who are waiting as well. Let it be known that if God has set a divine plan for you, it "shall" come to pass, because it's part of your purpose.

I want you to sit back and meditate on all that Ruth endured, from the beginning to the end, before her promise came. She didn't even know that Boaz was a part of her life when she was out in the fields of Moab, but destiny set her on the course. Many times we may be out there doing our own thing, while being stuck in Moab.

We're going from man to man but God pulls us into His bosom and sets us on the path to Bethlehem. You may have even let go of many who have been in your life and have lost hope in love.

Olivia Stith

You must keep the flame burning in your heart. Don't let anyone extinguish that fire that burns in you to be loved. All you have to do is trust that as you walk in the field to find your way to Bethlehem; He will keep you under His wings.

On your way to Bethlehem people will come into your life to make sure you stay on the right path. As for your Naomi's, stand with them and be loyal. Make sure you build them up as they guide you, for through your faithfulness your name will be established. Let your focus be on what God has called you to do in your life and not on a man. The man is there, but it's a transition that we all must go through. It's difficult, but it's life that through the power of the Holy Spirit you can live. You must live a life sold out for God in order for Him to set you in place for Boaz.

You may not see him or understand all you are going through but keep working in the field God has set you in. There is a divine reason that you are in the season you are.

God has someone out there looking at you while you are doing your Father's business. You best believe that! Not only are his eyes on you but the eyes of God as well.

You will know it because the favor of God will start to be manifested in your life and then that special man will appear. In the transition, you both may not know who you are, but God will reveal all things in His time. Enjoy the friendship and union of that special man, as God orchestrates His divine plan for both of you. It's His will for you to be connected divinely to one of His sons. So I pray that you keep the faith and keep working til the change comes. Remember, there is a man out there willing to give his all to have you because you are a divine daughter of the King. My Ruth sisters, keep the faith and you shall receive your promise. Boaz awaits you! I know, because God says so!

CHAPTER 24

In The Field Til A Change Comes

I've read the book of Ruth many times in my life but never as I have while writing this book. It was as though I was walking through her journey, in her body. It's then when I realized that the same Spirit that was driving her into her destiny and purpose is the same one today that is positioning me in the fields. The Spirit of God that was revealing His truths through her story was bringing something alive in mine. I pray the same has happened in your life as well my sister.

Let it be known that God has no respect of person that He is the same today, yesterday and forever more. This is why I had so much hope and joy in reading the book of Ruth and reliving the events of her life with Boaz.

I now see that God is the one who is faithful at keeping His promises in the midst of all that we have been through. The key thing is focusing on the call that He has in our life. It's obvious that God is one that works behind the scenes. Let's face it, we don't know what's best for us unless God guides us. This is so important in the preparation of being with our soul mate. The transition period is one that pulls at the very fiber of everything that holds us together as a woman. This is why we must stay in position and not move until God leads us.

It's evident that when we first cross paths with our Boaz, we won't know immediately. I have heard some men and women say they felt it in their spirit.

Hey, I can't say they didn't but I still believe it's a process that we must go through in order to bring the fullness of the relationship to the position that God will have it.

Olivia Stith

This requires so much patience and faith, that as I was reading the book, at times I found myself wondering, "when Lord, when?" That's our human nature. We know it's going to happen, but we don't know when. Then when it gets to the point of God confirming the person, we still must wait and that's a lot! We all know that patience is a requirement.

So now I implore you all to just sit back and look at your lives to evaluate what position or field you are in. Heaven forbid, if you are in Moab! Please pick up and leave immediately! That's not the place for you sister. Better days lie ahead for you. Christ has come so you can have life and have it more abundantly! Amen on that!

To my fellow servant girls who are in Bethlehem working the fields along with me, keep gleaning and working , you never know who is watching. Continue to keep the spirit of humility regardless of how hard things may appear in your life. This is only a temporary season. God is going to bring a refreshing in your life and He is going to feed you in a manner that you will grow with an overflow. Don't be weary my girlfriends, for in due season we shall reap. You are in this place for a reason. God is working behind the scenes and you never know who else is.

As long as we carry ourselves as holy, sanctified and strong women of God, men of God will come into our lives and show us favor. God himself has put that man in our life for a divine purpose. There is joy in knowing that by God's grace, all of our work is not in vain.

Olivia Stith

A Boaz will come in season and lift the load. Even for the men who may be in some of your lives, honor this man with your righteousness and know that all you do is for God's glory, not yours. God needs you to keep the faith in Him, so that your heart and motives remain pure. He will then reward you with the desires of your heart.

Keep in mind that there is a man out there walking with that spiritual rib missing from his side, which is you! Until that rib is put into place, he will continue to be out there seeking and watching those that come into his field. Remember not to fret and worry about anything, because when you step onto the scene he will know it's you. How will he know? He will know by the unique favor that God has placed on your life before him. Favor, favor that will ignite a fire only when he stands before God and looks you in the eyes and say, "I DO"!

Keep the faith. Boaz is on His way. In fact, he may be looking over your shoulder today. Happy harvesting and remain blessed.

10 Thoughts to Ponder

Here are a few questions to meditate on involving your personal development of being prepared to go through the transition of meeting your Boaz and becoming a wife. Take a moment to think on each question, write down your thoughts, and feel free to discuss them with your women's study group!

1. Our shortcomings do not have to be our downfall. If we recognize the areas in which we fall short, we can sit down and find solutions to develop them into strengths. Don't use your shortcomings or lack of ambition as excuses for failure. Use them as tools of motivation to better yourself.

2. What steps have you made in your life to let go of dead relationships and move forward? Have you changed the people you associate with? Have you taken more time to pray? Write down factors that keep you from turning back to your old way of thinking and in getting into relationships with men whom were undeserving of your love.

Olivia Stith

3. What are some characteristics you think a woman must possess in order to leave all she knows behind and press forward into unknown territory when God is leading her?

4. Do you have women or men in your life that you trust to give you wise advice concerning your relationships? What in their lives made you see them as possible spiritual mentors?

5. You are called for a purpose. What is your ministry/calling in the body of Christ? If you don't know, what are you doing to gain that knowledge? God has given each person He created special gifts and abilities to be used for kingdom building. Some gifts are more evident than others. The key thing is finding where your gift fits in the body of Christ and functioning in it in order to elevate His kingdom here on earth. These gifts cannot be bought but are instilled in you from birth by the Creator. Cultivate that gift and know that God has entrusted you to do a great work with your gift.

6. What are some of the things you feel a woman should have in order before she marries? Why are these things important? Preparation is everything. It's wise to start building on your foundation for marriage before the appointed day. Having all aspects of your life in order will help things flow more productively when you become one with your mate. Remember a wise woman builds her house ahead of time. Set your mind to preparing now.

7. What is your view on the state of single women who are in the church waiting on a mate? Do you feel today that too many of them are focusing on the wrong things in order to be in position for that special man? What are some of the shortcomings you see going on today in the area of a woman waiting on her soul mate?

8. The end of a relationship does not spell the end of us ever finding love. Whether someone walks out of our life or if we decide to end the relationship, see it as the season changing. It's good to reflect on the good and bad situations in the relationship in order to recognize how the next one can be a far better experience from the ones in the past.

Olivia Stith

Think about your last two failed relationships? Why did they fail? Were the reasons spiritual or perhaps financial? What are you doing now to stop the cycle of your past mindset?

9. Has God shown you anything about the man who He will be sending in your life (i.e. through a dream, you both crossed paths)? What are some factors that you will consider when a man approaches you and lets you know he is interested in you as a mate? What personality traits, economic status and such are you looking for, if any? Think on what steps you will take to ensure that he is the right one for you.

10. Take a moment one day and plan your wedding! That's right, get the colors picked out, make up a ceremony, do things that do not require money (at the moment), and then pray over it. Keep the faith that God will allow this dream to take place. Then step forth from that day on, believing soon God will have you standing before him as a bride.

About the Author: Elder Olivia Stith

Olivia Stith is the CEO of TriManna Productions, which is a multi-faceted ministry that is catered towards cultivating individuals in spiritual and natural relationships, through spoken, written and visual arts. Ms. Stith is on a mission to empower women to walk in the Spirit of excellence by applying kingdom principles to their spiritual and natural relationships. She wants women who are desiring a Godly mate to know - if you can't pray, you will never get a priest. If you can't labor and travail in the kingdom fields, you will never help him birth a vision. If you can't trust your heart to lay before him naked, He will never be able to cover you. Presently she is working on her next book, *"Tell Prince Charming to Keep That Slipper!"*

For more information on this Woman of God please contact:

Olivia Stith

Bookings/Speaking Engagements:
Melissa Johnson at
trimannapublishing@gmail.com

Personal Websites:

http://oliviastithministries.com
http://www.myspace.com/ladyhasflava

Notes